Handbook for Phase 1 habitat survey

- a technique for environmental audit

England Field Unit

Nature Conservancy Council

1990

Reprinted 1993 © JNCC 1993

# Contents

Page

## Part 1 Operational guidelines

1 Introduction — 7
    1.1 History of Phase 1 survey — 7
    1.2 Rationale of Phase 1 survey — 7
    1.3 Outline of methodology for Phase 1 survey — 8
    1.4 The purpose of Phase 1 survey — 8

2 Planning a Phase 1 survey — 9
    2.1 Choice of survey system — 9
    2.2 Use of aerial photography and satellite imagery — 9
    2.3 Choice of scale for mapping — 11
    2.4 Use of existing information — 11
    2.5 Use of public appeals — 11
    2.6 Survey preparation — 11
    2.7 Staffing requirements — 12
    2.8 Selection and training of surveyors — 14
    2.9 Equipment and office requirements — 14
    2.10 Transport requirements — 15
    2.11 Publicity — 15

3 Field and office procedures — 16
    3.1 Fieldwork organisation — 16
    3.2 Mapping in the field — 16
    3.3 Preparation of the final map — 16
    3.4 Reproduction of habitat maps — 18
    3.5 Measurement and analysis of habitat areas — 18
    3.6 Sampling procedures — 19
    3.7 Area estimation by the line-intercept method — 19
    3.8 Digitisation — 19
    3.9 Accuracy — 20
    3.10 Interpretation of Phase 1 survey maps — 20
    3.11 Evaluation — 21
    3.12 Use of hierarchical alphanumeric habitat codes — 22

4 Urban surveys — 23
    4.1 Choice of scale — 23
    4.2 Target notes — 23
    4.3 Habitat classification — 23
    4.4 Survey procedure — 24
    4.5 Phase 2 survey — 24

5 Using the colour code mapping system — 26
    5.1 Use of colour — 26
    5.2 Additonal codes — 26

6 Target notes — 27
    6.1 Importance of target notes — 27
    6.2 Target note content — 27
    6.3 Target note format — 27
    6.4 General descriptions — 28

7 Data storage — 29
    7.1 Survey products — 29
    7.2 Habitat maps — 29
    7.3 Habitat area data — 29
    7.4 Target notes — 29

| | | | |
|---|---|---|---|
| 8 | The survey report | | 30 |
| 9 | Comparison of Phase 1 survey classification with other classifications | | 31 |
| | 9.1 | The SSSI habitat mapping scheme and the NCC/RSNC classification | 31 |
| | 9.2 | The Draft Phase 1 Habitat Mapping Manual | 32 |
| | 9.3 | The National Vegetation Classification | 33 |

## Part 2 - Field manual  35

| | | |
|---|---|---|
| 1 | Habitat classification and coding | 37 |
| 2 | Habitat definitions | 38 |

| | | |
|---|---|---|
| A | Woodland and scrub | 38 |
| B | Grassland and marsh | 39 |
| C | Tall herb and fern | 41 |
| D | Heathland | 41 |
| E | Mire | 42 |
| F | Swamp, marginal and inundation | 44 |
| G | Open water | 45 |
| H | Coastland | 47 |
| I | Rock exposure and waste | 48 |
| J | Miscellaneous | 49 |

## Acknowledgements  50

## References  51

## Appendices

| | | |
|---|---|---|
| 1 | Phase 1 survey habitat classification, hierarchical alphanumeric reference codes and mapping colour codes | 53 |
| 2 | Habitat codes for use on monochrome field maps and fair maps | 61 |
| 3 | Dominant species codes | 64 |
| 4 | Key words and status categories for target notes | 67 |
| 5 | Hypothetical examples of target notes | 70 |
| 6 | Standard recording forms | 71 |
| 7 | The NCC/RSNC habitat classification | 75 |
| 8 | Relationship between Phase 1 habitat categories and National Vegetation Classification communities | 77 |

# Part 1
# Operational guidelines

# 1 Introduction

This manual presents a standardised system for classifying and mapping wildlife habitats in all parts of Great Britain, including urban areas. The manual provides information on the planning and execution of habitat surveys and is based on the experience of a large number of surveys which have been carried out in the past decade. It is hoped that this publication will facilitate the survey of the remaining areas of Britain. It would be of great benefit to nature conservation and to development planning if every local authority were in possession of a Phase 1 habitat survey and if a comprehensive Phase 1 survey database existed for each area of the country.

The Nature Conservancy Council (NCC) has played a leading role in devising and implementing standardised methods of biological survey and the NCC Phase 1 survey methodology has been widely used throughout Britain. It is very important that a standardised system is used and that surveys are carried out to a consistent level of detail and accuracy, so that the results of one survey may be compared with those of another and maps and statistical data may be readily interpreted.

## 1.1 History of Phase 1 survey

The origins of Phase 1 survey go back to the 1970s, when a system was devised for rapid mapping of wildlife habitats over large areas of countryside. The method was used originally in south-east Scotland and later in Cumbria and West Yorkshire. (NCC 1979a, 1979b).

After the passing of the Wildlife and Countryside Act 1981, this system was modified and extended for use in mapping habitats on Sites of Special Scientific Interest (SSSI) (NCC 1982, 1983a). The SSSI habitat mapping system was considered to be too detailed for use in Phase 1 surveys of the wider countryside and a simplified, but compatible, version was produced for this purpose (NCC 1983b). This version has been widely used for large-scale habitat surveys such as the Phase 1 Survey of Cumbria (NCC 1986a, Kelly & Perry 1990), although a number of large-scale surveys initiated before its publication (for example Somerset and Dorset - NCC 1983c, 1983d) used the full SSSI mapping system.

A draft manual on habitat survey was produced in 1986 (NCC 1986b) and this afforded an opportunity to clarify a number of habitat definitions and to make some minor changes in the habitat classification and coding. Although unpublished, this draft was widely circulated and has been used as the basis of most of the Phase 1 surveys of the late 1980s in England, Wales and Scotland.

The present manual is a revision of the 1986 draft and introduces further revisions of habitat definitions, mainly clarifying what has become accepted practice in existing survey but also introducing some changes in areas of ambiguity and confusion. In particular, the mires section has been revised, the dune classification has been simplified and the rather large semi-improved grassland category has been split into two, more functionally convenient, units. The classification covers the full range of terrestrial and intertidal habitats, but no attempt has been made to cover sub-tidal habitats.

Since 1982 all versions of the NCC Phase 1 habitat mapping system have been based on the same hierarchical classification system and are thus, in most respects, compatible with one another.

## 1.2 Rationale of Phase 1 survey

The aim of Phase 1 survey is to provide, relatively rapidly, a record of the semi-natural vegetation and wildlife habitat over large areas of countryside. The methodology presented in this manual is applicable both to surveys of specific habitats, such as grasslands or woodlands, and to surveys of the whole countryside, in which every parcel of land is classified and recorded. However, this manual is written largely with general surveys in mind, because these are more usual..

The habitat classification presented here is based principally on vegetation, augmented by reference to topographic and substrate features, particularly where vegetation is not the dominant component of the habitat. Vegetation is relatively simple to observe, identify and record and can thus be surveyed fairly rapidly over large areas without much difficulty. Because most animals are mobile, fugitive and small, they are often much more difficult to observe and record in the field, so comprehensive, large-scale faunal surveys are not a practical proposition.

The nature and condition of the vegetation embodies information about many of the living and non-living components of the environment. A study of the vegetation can thus provide an effective means of classifying and surveying habitats.

Ideally, a Phase 1 habitat survey should be followed up by a Phase 2 survey. This defines the vegetation of selected areas more precisely in terms of its plant communities, preferably as defined by the National Vegetation Classification, (Rodwell in prep.) and may include surveys of animal species and communities. Phase 2 survey can be used to describe the range of variation present for a particular habitat, thus indicating the representation required in the SSSI series. The sites at which Phase 2 surveys are to be targeted can be identified from the Phase 1 survey information. Occasionally it is desirable to carry out Phase 2 survey concurrently with Phase 1. A further stage in survey – Phase 3 – involves an even more detailed survey of the extent and distribution of plant and animal species on sites. The objective is to produce detailed information on the frequency or abundance of communities and species for site management and monitoring purposes. Information may be gathered on aspects such as the population size of individual species or their reproductive capacity.

## 1.3 Outline of methodology for Phase 1 survey

Briefly, the method of Phase 1 survey is as follows. Ideally every parcel of land in the entire survey area is visited by a trained surveyor and the vegetation is mapped on to Ordnance Survey maps, usually at a scale of 1:10,000, in terms of some ninety specified habitat types, using standard colour codes. In practice much of the mapping can be carried out from public rights of way, using binoculars at relatively short ranges to identify the vegetation. Aerial photographs may also be useful, especially in urban and in upland areas, as an adjunct to ground survey.

The use of colour codes on the final habitat maps allows rapid visual assessment of the extent and distribution of different habitat types. Further information is gained from the use of dominant species codes within many habitat types and from descriptive 'target notes' which give a brief account of particular areas of interest. The target notes are an essential part of Phase 1 survey and may provide the basis for selection of sites for Phase 2 survey and for decision-making in relation to conservation in the wider countryside.

Once mapped, the habitat areas are measured on the maps and statistics compiled on the extent and distribution of each habitat type. These statistics can then be held on computers.

The end products of a Phase 1 survey are (a) habitat maps, (b) target notes and (c) statistics. Ideally, the results should be supported by a descriptive and interpretative report. A descriptive summary for each Ordnance Survey map sheet has been found useful in some circumstances.

## 1.4 The purpose of Phase 1 survey

Nature conservation entails the conservation of wild plants and animals and natural and semi-natural habitats. It cannot be carried out effectively without a knowledge of the nature of these habitats and of their location, extent and distribution. The purpose of Phase 1 survey is to provide this information.

The availability of Phase 1 survey information in the form of coloured maps, target notes and statistics has been much appreciated by planners and conservationists and, where available, makes an almost daily contribution to the work of nature conservation. Even sites of relatively limited conservation interest may nevertheless be of strategic importance to nature conservation, acting for instance, as wildlife corridors or 'stepping stones'. These areas, as well as sites with more obvious wildlife value, and the relationships between them, can be clearly seen on the Phase 1 survey maps.

The information provided by Phase 1 survey has many uses for conservationists. It provides an objective basis for determining which sites warrant Phase 2 surveys and which sites deserve consideration for protection as SSSIs, Local Nature Reserves, local trust wildlife sites, etc. It gives a clearly defined baseline for monitoring change and embodies the information needed for the compilation of a habitat database for use in the conservation of the countryside.

Local authorities find Phase 1 survey of great value because it provides vital information needed in the formulation of policy, applied, for instance, in structure, local, subject and development plans or individual planning applications. The possession of a Phase 1 survey report allows planners to respond quickly to planning applications. It also strengthens the attitude of authorities, because the statistics it provides can be used to support the case for conservation of threatened habitats, especially in work connected with appeals. The information helps in the production and evaluation of environmental impact assessments and in the development of countryside strategies. Finally, Phase 1 survey can save time and money by providing knowledge that will enable planners and developers to avoid the controversy involved in environmental issues.

The early completion of nationwide surveys of biological features, for the purpose of identifying all those areas which qualify for protection and wildlife management, is a priority objective in *Nature conservation in Great Britain* (NCC, 1984). Phase 1 survey is the most suitable vehicle available for accomplishing this task.

# 2 Planning a Phase 1 survey

## 2.1 Choice of survey system

It is generally considered that no real choice exists as to the method of collecting Phase 1 survey information since there is no satisfactory alternative to the inspection of each habitat unit in the field by a trained surveyor. The use of remote sensing techniques such as aerial photography and satellite imagery would appear to be a much more cost-effective way of surveying large areas of land but these methods have not yet been proved capable of distinguishing the full range of habitat categories required for Phase 1 survey in Britain. Although further technological improvements may, in time, achieve this capability, remote sensing methods will probably never be able to supply the level of detail available from ground survey and will, in any case, always rely on ground survey for verification.

## 2.2 Use of aerial photography and satellite imagery

Although aerial photography is no substitute for fieldwork in Phase 1 survey, the availability of contemporary aerial photographic coverage at a suitable scale (from 1:5,000 to 1:12,000) can greatly increase the speed and facility with which field survey is carried out. Aerial photographs, preferably in colour, should be procured where available.

It must be stressed that some habitat types are difficult or impossible to distinguish on aerial photographs and that habitats which are uncommon and of small extent, and therefore likely to be of high conservation value, may be overlooked.

Aerial photography has been found to be most useful for:-

- providing an overview of an area prior to survey;

- mapping habitats in areas of restricted or difficult access, where these may be directly compared with similar habitats in the neighbouring area;

- picking out areas of high arable intensity;

- determining the boundaries of well defined habitat units which are not apparent from the Ordnance Survey map (for example woodlands, plantation, fellings, quarries, housing estates and new industrial development);

- pinpointing areas of broadleaved woodland in conifer plantations (or vice-versa);

- picking out undeveloped sites in urban areas;

- determining the boundaries between adjacent habitats where these do not correspond to any feature on the Ordnance Survey map (for example a boundary between blanket bog and acid grassland in the uplands);

- checking the alignments of recent road-building developments, although this is probably best achieved using plans from the council highway department.

The value of aerial photographs is limited primarily by the quality and age of the photographs and by scale. The ease of interpretation also depends on the season of year and time of day that they were taken, because shadows greatly alter the look of vegetation. Winter photographs can be difficult to interpret because of the lack of vegetation cover.

At a scale of 1:5,000, species of broadleaved trees can be distinguished by crown shape and every habitat feature of sufficient size can be recognised using a stereoscope. Distinctions can be made between most of the habitats recognised in this manual, although the grassland type (calcareous, neutral, acidic) would be inferred from local knowledge rather than from the aerial photograph itself. Topography can be clearly seen using a stereoscope and this too helps to distinguish features such as unimproved calcareous grassland on slopes too steep to 'improve'. Certain species (for example of *Nardus*, *Molinia* and *Juncus*) are easily distinguished on aerial photographs and this can help in identifying grassland types in upland areas.

Aerial photographic survey is a useful means of monitoring changes in the distribution and abundance of specific habitat types such as broadleaved woodland, hedges or heathland. Studies carried out using the aerial photography of the 1940s and 1970s indicate the scale of habitat loss during that period and form the basis of the National Countryside Monitoring Scheme (NCC 1980, 1987, 1988).

The two main types of satellite imagery which can be used most effectively for habitat mapping are LANDSAT Thematic Mapper (LANDSAT TM) images, with 30 m resolution capability, and the SPOT system, which has resolution capabilities down to 10 m. However, neither system provides images of the quality needed for the whole range of habitats mapped at Phase 1. These techniques produce images corresponding to the reflectance recorded in certain wavelengths of light, including the infra-red band, enabling vegetation to be distinguished from buildings, etc. In the SPOT system, despite the greater spatial resolution, the spectral resolution is less good than with LANDSAT TM. However, texture is more obvious with SPOT images. No species list can be compiled. Because remote sensing techniques depend on intensity of reflection, certain habitat types such as scrub may be overlooked if the area of scrub is scattered over grassland, since each pixel of the image displays an average intensity for the vegetation present. In this respect, it should also be noted that small habitat areas (less than 10 x 10 m for SPOT and less than 30 x 30 m for LANDSAT TM) may be overlooked entirely.

Satellite imagery can be valuable in monitoring land use change, as, for example, in a study of an area of marsh pastureland in East Anglia (Baker & Drummond 1984). Here, data from LANDSAT were successfully used to pinpoint pasture fields which had been converted to arable land over the course of a decade.

If remote sensing techniques are used it is strongly recommended that ground truth exercises are carried out to check the accuracy of interpretation.

The relative advantages and disadvantages of ground survey, aerial photography and satellite imagery are summarised in Table 1.

## Table 1   Comparison of Phase 1 survey with remote sensing methods

| Phase 1 survey | Aerial photography | Satellite imagery |
|---|---|---|
| Complete ground cover possible; not limited by availability of other data | Complete cover exists for 1940s; cover good for 1970s but incomplete for other dates; quality variable | Frequent complete cover exists since 1982 for LANDSAT TM, but cloud obscures many images |
| Direct recording in the field | Relies on tone and pattern of spectral reflectance | Relies on spectral reflectance in a more limited range of tones, but images have greater contrast than for aerial photography |
| Accuracy depends on skill of field surveyors; few problems of interpretation | Image accurate but interpretation variable and often difficult | Image accurate; interpretation by specialists essential |
| Can be used to standardise other methods | Should be calibrated by field survey | Should be calibrated by field survey |
| No sophisticated or expensive equipment | Needs complicated and expensive equipment | Needs sophisticated and expensive equipment |
| Yields complete set of Phase 1 habitat categories | Yields limited set of habitat categories | Yields limited set of habitat categories |
| Yields maps, descriptive notes and statistical data | Can yield maps and statistical data | Can yield maps and statistical data |
| Gives information on dominant and other plant species | Little species information | Very little species information |
| Gives information on canopy and groundlayer | Information on canopy only (unless repeated at different seasons) | Information on canopy only (unless repeated at different seasons) |
| Data gathering slow, interpretation rapid | Data gathering quick, but interpretation laborious | Data gathering quick; interpretation potentially very fast if fully automated |
| Target notes give site-related information on species, communities, management, threats, etc for a large number of sites | Site-related information limited; no target notes | Site-related information limited; no target notes |
| Can be used for conservation evaluation | Limited use for conservation evaluation | Limited use for conservation evaluation |

## 2.3  Choice of scale for mapping

Those planning Phase 1 rural surveys are faced with the choice of using either 1:10,000 or 1:25,000 scale Ordnance Survey maps. To date, county-wide Phase 1 surveys have been carried out at either 1:10,000 or 1:25,000 scale but there has been an increasing tendency to standardise on a scale of 1:10,000 despite some of the advantages of the smaller scale. The choice of scale for urban surveys is discussed in Section 4.1.

1:10,000 scale maps cost more than 1:25,000 maps and four times as many sheets are required to cover a given area. The large number of much larger maps is less convenient to store, more time-consuming to produce and more costly to reproduce. The area used to represent a given unit of land on a 1:10,000 scale map is 6.25 times that on a 1:25,000 scale map. However, the cost of purchasing maps is small compared with the cost of the surveyors' time and the larger 1:10,000 scale allows habitats to be mapped in greater detail and provides space for the inclusion of dominant species codes. At 1:25,000 scale, the minimum mappable area is approximately 0.5 ha, whereas at 1:10,000 scale habitat units down to 0.1 ha can be mapped routinely and smaller habitats, such as ponds, may also be mapped.

There is no doubt that for use in relation to planning matters a 1:10,000 scale is desirable, but it is recognised that for very large areas such as the Scottish Highlands a 1:25,000 scale survey may be the only economically feasible choice. The habitat codes presented in this manual are suitable for use at either scale. Where survey is carried out at 1:25,000 scale, it is recommended that full use is made of target notes to provide greater detail in the survey.

## 2.4  Use of existing information

Existing information relevant to Phase 1 survey may take many forms.

Examples are:-

maps and descriptive information from previous habitat surveys of all or part of the survey area, including detailed information on Sites of Special Scientific Interest;

maps and descriptions of sites of local wildlife interest, usually held by the county wildlife trust;

records relating to specific habitats at a limited number of sites, or more extensive habitat-specific surveys (for example woodland, meadow, lakeshore or riverbank surveys);

records of ornithological and other species surveys which may be general or restricted to selected sites;

Biological Recording Centre (BRC) cards and other species lists relating to specific sites.

All these data should be made available to the surveyor and summarised in the form of grid-referenced target notes. These should be indicated on the field maps for easy reference during the field survey. Wherever possible or relevant, the surveyor should attempt to update the existing information, verifying its present status in the field and noting any change or loss (or lack of change). Existing information should not be used as a substitute for current survey but where incorporated it should be dated and attributed.

## 2.5  Use of public appeals

The use of public appeals as a means of ascertaining the whereabouts of specific habitats has been suggested and may be particularly useful in locating herb-rich grasslands (see NCC 1977) but caution should be exercised in their use. Like other sources of existing information they may be a useful addition to field survey but are no substitute for it and consideration must be given to the time involved in dealing with the members of the public who provide information. This said, the more local knowledge surveyors can acquire, the more effective their survey is likely to be.

## 2.6  Survey preparation

The work programme should be planned carefully at the beginning of the survey so as to cover the survey area within the field season. There is much to be said for working systematically over the area, completing one map at a time so that no gaps are left. However, some habitats are best surveyed at different times of year from others - woodlands in spring, grasslands in mid-summer, heathlands in autumn, open waters between mid-June and the end of September. To survey an area one habitat at a time in this fashion is likely to be time-consuming and costly, involving repeated visits to each locality. A reasonable compromise would be to select for survey in spring and early summer those areas most rich in woodlands, to survey in midsummer those areas most likely to have semi-natural grasslands and to leave areas of moorland until later in the field season. Within these selected areas, all habitats should be surveyed at the same time, although some may be noted as requiring further survey at a later (or earlier) period of the year.

The field season should be considered as starting in late March/early April in the south and late April/early May in the north of England. The season generally ends about mid-October, although in a mild season it may be possible to carry out some survey in November. Except perhaps in the uplands, such end-of-season field survey should be restricted to checking areas surveyed earlier, and must be pursued with caution since many plant species will no longer be apparent. For safety reasons the field season may be curtailed in upland areas. It is important to set aside sufficient time during the winter period to complete the production of maps and target notes, the measurement and analysis of the maps and the writing and production of a report.

It is important to allow time prior to the field season for planning and preparation. The more that is accomplished before the field season gets underway, the more successful the survey will be.

Items on which time should be spent prior to the field season are:-

planning the field survey;

recruiting and training surveyors and ancillary staff (for example cartographers and typists);

providing office accommodation, equipment and clothing for the team;

compiling existing survey information;

preparing field maps.

## 2.7 Staffing requirements

The main areas of work entailed in Phase 1 survey are as follows:-

supervision, co-ordination and administration

field survey and target note production;

fair and master map production;

measurement and analysis of habitat areas;

report production.

Staff will, of course, have to be taken on to cover all these requirements, but the availability of resources and personnel have varied so much in the past (and will no doubt continue to do so in the future) that little guidance can be given on recruitment.

Experience suggests that full-time supervisory posts are essential for smooth and efficient operation and to co-ordinate team effort. The maximum number of surveyors per supervisor should be seven.

Surveyor fieldwork rates depend on many factors, including the relative competence of individual surveyors, whether they operate singly or in pairs, whether surveying is continued into the winter, the topography, complexity, interest and accessibility of the area to be surveyed and the scale at which mapping is carried out. As a rough guide, the work involved in surveying, producing and analysing a single 1:10,000 scale habitat map (5 x 5 km) is shown below, in Table 2. For most 1:10,000 scale habitat surveys it would be reasonable to expect each surveyor to produce 10 map sheets of completed survey per year.

| Table 2 | Approximate time needed for each 1:10,000 scale habitat map (5 x 5 km) |
|---|---|
| Field survey and production of fair copy | 8-10 days |
| Production of final copy from fair copy | 1½-2½ days |
| Analysis of final copy using dot grid | 1-1½ days |

Rates based on Phase 1 surveys of Cumbria and Lancashire, 1983-1988.

Table 3 presents average fieldwork rates from a number of different surveys and can be used to give an indication of likely manpower requirements. It is apparent from Table 3 that survey rates vary considerably from one area to another depending upon the terrain, the amount of interest and the scale spending approximately two days per week on this task and writing up target notes. In the Dorset survey it took about 16 hours per 1:25,000 sheet to copy fair colour maps. In the Norfolk survey it took about 8 hours per 1:10,000 sheet to prepare monochrome fair maps from field maps.

Table 3  Average fieldwork rates for ten Phase 1 surveys (including fair map production)

| Survey | Map scale | Cartographic assistance | Winter surveying | Survey rate per surveyor km²/day | km²/year |
|---|---|---|---|---|---|
| Dorset | 1:25,000 | No | No | 5.5 | 500 |
| Somerset | 1:25,000 | No | No | 6.4 | 580 |
| Devon and Cornwall | 1:10,000 | No | No | c.6 | 310 |
| Cumbria | 1:10,000 | Yes | No | 3.0 | 270 |
| Wales | 1:10,000 | No | No | 2.5 | 240 |
| Norfolk | 1:10,000 | Yes | Yes | - | 670 |
| Nottingham | 1:10,000 | No | No | 2.4 | 200 |
| Yorkshire Dales National Park | 1:10,000 | No | No | 1.6 | - |
| N York Moors | 1:10,000 | No | No | 0.8 | 81 |
| London, GLC/LWT | 1:10,000 | Yes | Yes | - | 537 |

of the survey. One remarkably constant result is that the total area covered by each surveyor in a year is approximately 90 times the daily survey rate (except where survey was continued through the winter), thus one can estimate on the basis of 90 field survey days per year.

The following examples give some idea of the staffing needed for map production. In the Greater London Council/London Wildlife Trust habitat survey of Greater London a single cartographer was able to cope with the input from five surveyors preparing coloured fair maps from field maps. In the Dorset, Somerset and Cumbria surveys, surveyors prepared their own fair maps,

With regard to the measurement of habitat areas, in the Dorset survey it took roughly 10 hours to measure each habitat parcel within a 1:25,000 scale sheet, using an electronic planimeter. In the Norfolk survey, it took about 8 hours to do the same for a 1:10,000 scale sheet, using a graphic digitising tablet linked to a micro-computer. In Cumbria it took 20 hours to measure all habitat areas on a 1:10,000 scale sheet using a Romer dot grid.

Adequate time must be set aside for producing the survey report (see Section 8).

## 2.8 Selection and training of surveyors

Surveyors should be taken on by early March in order to complete training for fieldwork beginning in April. Ideally, each surveyor should be a competent botanist with a keenness for accurate field recording and mapping. Familiarity with the use of large scale maps, the ability to work independently in the field and a readiness to make decisions are all advantageous. A personality suited to negotiating and liaising with landowners is desirable. A driving licence may be essential. Writing and numerical skills will be needed for the production of target notes and reports, and the ability to produce neat final maps is essential when cartographers are not employed. Willingness to work away from the base, possibly for extended periods during the field season, is advantageous. It must be remembered that the work is physically demanding and surveyors should be fit and healthy. Conscientiousness, enthusiasm and reliability all make for a good surveyor.

The use of volunteers can be less than satisfactory since they may not be available at the time the survey needs their help. Also, until they are thoroughly trained they are of limited use to the survey and must therefore be regarded as a last resort. The use of volunteers for cartographic assistance is a possibility, but careful supervision is needed.

It is essential that surveyors are adequately trained to ensure accuracy and consistency both within and between surveys. Discrepancies between the work of different surveyors and between different surveys can be reduced if surveyors are trained to a uniform standard, as laid out in this manual. The amount of training necessary will depend on the experience of the surveyors, but generally an initial period of 2 weeks in the field will be the minimum requirement, with frequent further training, monitoring and refresher sessions throughout the field season. During the initial training the team should operate as a group so that general agreement may be reached on how to deal with any problems that may arise. Particular attention should be paid to the habitat classification and trainers should attempt to visit the full range of habitats likely to be encountered, including some samples of species-rich sites.

Training should cover the field identification of the full range of vascular plants likely to be encountered in the area of the survey (flowering plants, including grasses, sedges and rushes, also ferns and club mosses). The field identification of bog-mosses *Sphagnum* spp is important in identifying mire habitats and should be included if possible.

Training should also be given in other fieldwork skills such as the use of binoculars in vegetation survey, mapping techniques, navigation and route-finding, planning a day's survey, negotiating access, habitat identification, indications of trophic status, soils, management and writing target notes. The amount of detail to be recorded must be made clear to surveyors and they should be made aware of their expected rate of progress.

Even after initial training, surveyors should be encouraged to bring back plant specimens to the office for identification or checking and should report the whereabouts of any problematic habitats, so that these can be reviewed and classified by the whole team, seeking outside advice as necessary. Under the Wildlife and Countryside Act 1981, it is an offence to uproot wild plants without the authority of the owner or occupier. Surveyors should follow the BSBI (Botanical Society of the British Isles) Code of Conduct.

To ensure consistency throughout the country, trainers should, ideally, have some experience of other Phase 1 surveys. Likewise it is very useful for survey supervisors to meet together at the beginning and end of the field season in order to share ideas, solve problems and maintain uniform standards of survey.

## 2.9 Equipment and office requirements

### 2.9.1 Personal equipment

Each surveyor will require the following items:-

    identity card and code of conduct

    waterproof jacket and overtrousers

    wellington boots and walking boots

    compass

    binoculars (8 x 30)

    clipboard (A3 or A4)

    large plastic bags (for protection of maps, notebooks etc in wet weather)

    botanical field guides, including *Excursion flora* (3rd ed.) (Clapham *et al.* 1981) and/or *Flora of the British Isles* (3rd ed.) (Clapham *et al.* 1987)

    hand lens (x10)

    1:50,000 Ordnance Survey maps

    1:10,000 or 1:25,000 (copy) field maps

    coloured pencils, lead pencils, rubber, notebook

    first aid kit

    whistle

    survival bag if working in remote or mountainous country

    field manual section of *Handbook for Phase 1 habitat survey*;

insect repellant and sun-tan lotion, if needed.

hand-held radios for person-to-person communication during fieldwork are recommended for use by surveyors. They are useful for morale and safety as well as being a valuable means of altering plans during the day (for example when access permission is refused). Personal alarms should be available to those who wish to carry them.

### 2.9.2 Office equipment

The following items should be provided for use in the office:-

- line hatching apparatus (optional)
- planimeter (optional)
- Romer dot grids for measuring areas and determining grid references
- T-squares, set squares, rulers
- pocket calculators
- stationery: pens, pencils, paper, etc.
- Rotring drawing pens (0.35 mm, 0.5 mm)
- Berol Verithin coloured pencils
- full version of *Handbook for Phase 1 habitat survey*

### 2.9.3 Maps and aerial photographs

Complete coverage of the survey area is needed at 1:50,000 and 1:10,000 (or 1:25,000) scale. Geological maps and soil maps are valuable aids to habitat mapping and should be available in the office if possible.

Aerial photographs, particularly recent colour photography, are very useful (see Section 2.2). If aerial photographs are to be taken into the field, commercially available transparent protective envelopes should be used.

### 2.9.4 Other items

In addition to the above equipment, photocopying, typing and map storage facilities will be required. Photocopying machines must be of high quality so that maps are copied with the minimum of distortion.

A range of text books on relevant specialist topics, including standard floras and identification guides, should be available.

### 2.9.5 Office space

Offices must be well-lit, and a working surface of 1x2m should be available for each surveyor. If the area to be surveyed is large, then it may be deemed desirable to use several widely separated offices, each with overnight accommodation available nearby, in order to minimize the time spent travelling and to reduce transport costs. In the Phase 1 survey of Cumbria, it was found worthwhile to limit the maximum distance between office and survey area to 50 km.

## 2.10 Transport requirements

The surveyors will require almost continuous access to motor vehicles during the field season, preferably with not less than one car to two surveyors. After salaries, transport will be the most expensive item on any Phase 1 budget. Areas close to the surveyors' homes or to the office may be visited on foot or by bicycle but access to all other areas must be by car, except for the occasional train or bus journey. The North Wales Phase 1 team used a combination of a car and a bicycle; driving to the area of survey and dropping off one surveyor with a bike for the day to be picked up later on. This worked well and reduced costs considerably. Table 4 gives an indication of the likely total distance.

**Table 4 Total distance travelled by car in four Phase 1 surveys**

| Survey | Area surveyed (km$^2$) | Distance travelled (km) |
| --- | --- | --- |
| Dorset | 2700 | 17,669 |
| Somerset | 2920 | 21,440 |
| N York Moors | 325 | 11,400 |
| Nottingham | 1800 | 23,000 |

## 2.11 Publicity

It is strongly recommended that details of any forthcoming survey are published in the local farming press, with a request for co-operation and an address to which enquiries may be directed. Advice should be sought from local branches of the National Farmers' Union and County Landowners' Association as to appropriate papers or journals. Coverage on local television should also be considered. Such publicity has in the past been found valuable in helping landowners and occupiers to consider requests for access permission in a favourable light and reducing unfounded accusations of trespass or 'spying'. It also prepares the farming community to accept survey results such as figures on the extent of remaining semi-natural habitat.

County (or Regional in Scotland) and District Councils should be approached during the initial stages of planning of any survey, and asked to endorse the proposals. They may be able to use their powers under the 1971 Town and Country Planning Act (Section 280) to provide access for the purpose of survey, especially if they are funding the survey.

# 3 Field and office procedures

## 3.1 Fieldwork organisation

For reasons of safety, consistency and transport economy, it is suggested that surveyors operate in pairs, surveying separate areas in the field but remaining in loose contact, to ensure that the ground is completely covered and to guard against accident. Such daily contact also helps to maintain consistency of work to resolve minor difficulties and to maintain morale.

Surveying should be carried out from roads, footpaths and other public rights of way wherever possible, using binoculars where necessary and only resorting to the time-consuming process of seeking access permission where no such rights of way exist. Trespass should be avoided at all times. Aerial photographs can be used to map areas of difficult or restricted access and also for mapping the interiors of large woods (see Section 2.1). Indeed, it may be a good idea to take aerial photographs into the field, where they can also be used for on-the-spot comparison with Ordnance Survey maps, for checking boundaries etc. However, aerial photographs are expensive and their owners may be reluctant for them to be taken out of the office.

Owners of large estates, or their agents, should be approached well in advance by letter or telephone for access permission, but a personal visit from the surveyor on the day of the survey is normally sufficient to secure access to most farms.

Each day's fieldwork should be carefully planned to maximise the amount of ground covered and to minimise overlap and back-tracking. Care should be taken to ensure that the whole landscape is covered, and that no gaps are left which will necessitate a further visit to the area. Drop-off and pick-up points and times must be agreed upon and surveyors' routes marked on their field maps. For safety reasons a daily itinerary and route map should also be left with someone at the office or place of accommodation.

In hilly terrain, it is often advantageous to start the day's surveying by making a preliminary inspection with binoculars from a vantage point, to identify land use patterns and field boundary changes and to locate potentially interesting sites and eliminate arable areas which can be mapped from that point. Binoculars are also extremely valuable at short range. They are essential for examining fields from gateways and footpaths in order to determine the species diversity in the main body of the field. With practice, many plant species can be reliably identified from a distance.

In preparation for a day's fieldwork, surveyors should mark up their maps with appropriate information such as the boundaries of the day's survey, the location of SSSIs and reserves and previous survey data.

## 3.2 Mapping in the field

Each distinct habitat unit is recorded in the field using coloured pencils (see Appendix 1) or, alternatively, lettered codes or alphanumeric codes (Appendix 2) in pencil or ink. Colours and codes should be entered directly onto copies of the large scale (normally 1:10,000) Ordnance Survey maps. These copies are usually paper photocopies, but dyeline copies on polyester sheet and photocopies on waterproof paper have also been used. Waterproof paper, though expensive, is useful in wet conditions. Whichever method of copying is chosen, it is essential to check that the contour lines are visible on the copies, as these are often needed in field mapping.

There are advantages in mapping directly in colour in the field but some surveys have chosen to use pen or pencil only, mapping the habitat boundaries and using the mnemonic lettered codes or the hierarchical alphanumeric codes to identify the habitat types (see Appendix 2). This is quicker and more convenient, particularly in wet weather and in recording uncomplicated situations. The use of colour is preferable in complex situations and where there are large amounts of semi-natural vegetation, but the maps must be kept dry as the colours run when wet.

From the point of view of accuracy and consistency it is important to standardise on the minimum size of habitat unit to be mapped. It is suggested that at 1:10,000 scale all habitat units larger than 0.1 ha should be mapped and at 1:25,000 scale all units larger than 0.5 ha, although it is possible to map smaller units, for instance ponds. The mapping of features which cross boundaries must be standardised, to facilitate the preparation of a database.

Dominant species should be recorded wherever feasible using the species codes given in Appendix 3.

## 3.3 Preparation of final map

The procedure for preparation of final maps has varied from one survey to another, but the final objective in each case is to produce an accurate, full-colour habitat map – the master map – which has a high visual impact and is easy to interpret. The example printed with Appendix 1 is one of the final maps for the Leighton Buzzard area, taken from the Phase 1 habitat survey of Bedfordshire (Moreau in prep.).

Information may be transferred from field maps to fair maps either by surveyors themselves or by cartographers employed specifically for that purpose. Surveyors are likely to perform the task more precisely because of their familiarity with the actual ground situation, whilst cartographic staff are likely to produce more consistent and neater maps. Without doubt, employment of cartographers in addition to surveyors will make better use of the skills of the latter. If surveyors do prepare field maps themselves, experience suggests that the maps should be transferred within 3 days of being in the field, but if their target notes are good, they should be able to leave the mapping exercise a little longer. The same holds true for any other site-related information, but this must be carefully weighed against the surveyors' individual abilities and experience.

To reduce colour-fading to a minimum, maps should be stored in light-proof cabinets. Dyeline copies, which fade and change colour even in the dark, should not be used for master maps.

Three systems of mapping are compared in Table 5. In the north-west and south-west England surveys, the surveyors produced an accurate, coloured fair copy from their field maps, on another photocopy of the Ordnance Survey map. The final map was prepared by cartographers working from this fair copy, marking-up and colouring-in the original large scale Ordnance Survey map. Duplicate copies are made on 35 mm transparencies or full colour photocopies, as required.

In Wales, the coloured master map was prepared by the surveyors on a plastic paper photocopy of the Ordnance Survey map and a full-colour paper photocopy of this is made as a duplicate for safety purposes. In addition, a clear acetate dyeline copy of the Ordnance Survey map is coded in black ink so that monochrome photocopies can be produced.

In surveys where a black and white field map has been produced the information on this is traced carefully onto a clear acetate photocopy of the original Ordnance Survey map, using a Rotring pen. Paper photocopies of this monochrome map can be readily made as required. One such photocopy is coloured in to produce the coloured master map.

### Table 5  Three alternative schemes for producing habitat maps

A     Cumbria, Dorset and Somerset surveys
B     Norfolk and Greater London Council/London Wildlife Trust surveys
C     North Wales survey

| A | B | C |
|---|---|---|
| Field map (colour) | Field map (monochrome) | Field map (colour) |
| Paper photocopy of OS map with habitats coloured in by surveyors | Paper photocopy of OS map with habitat boundaries marked in and each habitat or parcel given a numerical or alphabetical code, in ink or pencil | Dyeline copy on polyester paper of OS map coloured in by surveyors |
| Fair map (colour) | Fair map (monochrome) | Fair map (monochrome) |
| Paper photocopy with habitats neatly coloured in. Habitat boundaries and species codes in black ink. | Photocopy of OS map on clear acetate with habitat boundaries and codes neatly drawn in black ink. Black and white photocopies as required. | Dyeline copy of OS map, on clear acetate, habitat-coded in black ink. Black and white photocopies as required. |
| Master map (colour) | Master map (colour) | Master map (colour and monochrome) |
| Hand-coloured (by cartographer) on the original OS map for definitive use. Colour photocopies as required | Habitats coloured in on one or more photo-copies of the fair map | Photocopy of OS map on plastic paper is colour-coded and species-coded. A colour photocopy of this map is made for security |

## 3.4 Reproduction of habitat maps

Habitat maps are most conveniently reproduced, whether in whole or in part, by photocopying, either in colour or black and white. The increasing availability and decreasing cost of colour photocopying facilities allows the use of full colour copies and extracts of habitat maps for working purposes in preference to black and white copies, except where large numbers are needed.

As noted in the previous section, a monochrome copy of the master map, most conveniently prepared by tracing onto clear acetate sheet, allows black and white photocopies to be made as required.

Permission must be obtained before photocopying and the copies should carry a notice declaring that the maps are based on the Ordnance Survey, with permission, and reserving the copyright.

It is important to keep a duplicate set of the final hand-coloured master maps and this may be done using 35mm transparencies or full-colour photocopies. Laser photocopiers can now produce accurate, full-size, full-colour copies (usually on A3 paper) at less than £10.00 per 1:10,000 map sheet. 35mm transparencies, mounted on microfiches, cost only 50 pence, but require a microfiche reader for use. They are easily stored and provide a useful back-up system in case of loss or damage of the originals.

## 3.5 Measurement and analysis of habitat areas

Measurement of the extent of each of the different types of habitat in the area covered by the survey represents one of the most useful analyses that can be carried out on the Phase 1 habitat maps, so this should be regarded as an essential part of the Phase 1 survey.

Statistics of the total amount of semi-natural habitat remaining and of the total area of each habitat type, expressed as a percentage of the survey area or as a percentage of the total semi-natural area, may be used effectively to demonstrate the status of a given habitat type in the survey area and to support the case for protection of habitats which are most endangered. Such habitat statistics also provide a valuable baseline for monitoring future change in the countryside.

In order to simplify the task of measuring habitat areas, it is suggested that the 90 or so different habitat categories given in the Phase 1 classification are combined as shown in Table 6, to give 34 categories for measurement. Consistent use of the groups will facilitate the generation of regional and national statistics on habitat extent. It may occasionally be desirable to measure areas at a finer level than indicated, but the measurements produced should be capable of being totalled to produce figures in line with the categories listed in Table 6.

---

**Table 6    Recommended grouping of habitats for area measurement**

---

Woodland and scrub
    Semi-natural broadleaved woodland
    Semi-natural coniferous woodland
    Semi-natural mixed woodland
    Plantation woodland (broadleaved, coniferous and mixed)
    Dense/continuous scrub
    Recently-felled woodland

Grassland
    Acid grassland (unimproved and semi-improved)
    Neutral grassland (unimproved and semi-improved)
    Calcareous grassland (unimproved and semi-improved)
    Improved + poor semi-improved grassland
    Marsh/marshy grassland

Tall herb and fern
    Continuous bracken
    All other tall herb and fern habitats

Heathland
    Acid + basic dry dwarf shrub heath + lichen/bryophyte heath + montane heath/dwarf forb
    Wet dwarf shrub heath
NB For mosaics classify as heath or grass according to majority cover. If proportion is unknown, divide 50/50.

Mire
    Blanket bog
    Raised bog
    Modified bog (wet and dry)
    Acid + basic flush
    Fen (valley + basin + flood-plain mires)

Swamp, marginal and inundation
    All types should be combined

Open water
    Standing water (all types, including coastal lagoons)
    Running water (all types)

Coastland
    Intertidal mud/sand (with or without *Zostera* or algal beds)
    Intertidal shingle/cobbles + boulders/rocks (with or without *Zostera* or algal beds)
    Dense/continuous saltmarsh
    Shingle + boulders/rocks above high tide mark + strandline vegetation
    All sand dune habitats
    All maritime cliff and slope habitats

Rock exposure
    All natural types, except limestone pavement
    Limestone pavement
    All artificial and waste types

Miscellaneous
    All cultivated/disturbed land
    All built-up areas

Where possible, area measurements should be made on the original Ordnance Survey map rather than on a photocopy. If a photocopy is used, area measurements should be corrected for any magnification error present. It should be noted that as a result of paper stretch in the copying machine, this error may be different along and across the grain of the paper. Despite the fact that hillsides will be under-measured, no attempt should be made to adjust areas for slope. The procedure is time-consuming and prone to error and the resulting correction is only significant in mountainous areas, where the method is inapplicable for other reasons.

The areas of plots should be measured using a Romer dot grid. Planimeters are not sufficiently accurate for the measurement of small areas. Measurements should be recorded on specially designed forms so that data may be readily retrieved and manipulated. This may be done most conveniently if the data are subsequently entered into a suitable computer file. It is then a simple matter to calculate such parameters as the average size, or the size-class distribution, of woodland or heathland habitat units in the county, the number of habitat blocks larger than 1 km$^2$, or the proportion of the total unimproved grassland in the county occurring within a particular district.

It is not considered practical to calculate the area of hedges, the width of which is over-represented by the coloured line on the map. Their abundance is best expressed as a linear measurement and most easily obtained from aerial photographs. In Phase 1 survey, the area of the hedge or other boundary is included in the area of the habitat unit which it bounds. Similarly, most road verges, railway cuttings and embankments, should, if measured, be expressed as length, but verges wider than 25 m should be included in area measurements for grassland or scrub, as appropriate.

Ditches, streams and rivers are also best represented by a linear measurement, but rivers exceeding 25 m in width, that is 2.5 mm at 1:10,000 scale, are included in area measurements as running water. The total area of road may be considerable, though much of it may lie within the built-up areas.

## 3.6 Sampling procedures

Although it is strongly recommended that all habitat areas are measured as described above, if resources are severely limited it is possible to obtain estimates of habitat abundance by the use of sampling procedures. However, great care is required in the design and use of sampling strategies, since habitats are invariably distributed in a non-random fashion. If sampling is contemplated, expert advice should be sought on suitable stratification procedures. Even with such procedures, it is difficult to produce reliable estimates for rare and localised habitats which are, by their nature, readily over- or under-sampled. Analysis of variance should be carried out in order to estimate the error in the area estimates, but it should be remembered that the reliability of this estimate is also sensitive to the sampling procedure.

A simple procedure which copes well with poorly dispersed samples is the line-intercept method (see 3.7), though it is somewhat sensitive to habitat size and will underestimate those habitats which are both small and rare. It is most accurate for the most abundant habitats and provides a convenient method of calculating the proportions of improved grassland and arable land in areas with large blocks of mixed agricultural land.

## 3.7 Area estimation by the line-intercept method

In this method the habitat map is sampled by a series of parallel line-transects to estimate the percentage cover of each habitat type (see Canfield 1941). The proportion of the map area covered by each habitat type is given by the total transect length falling within that habitat. Ideally, the transect lines should be parallel offsets at random intervals, but in practice, provided that the habitat patches are not regularly distributed, a good estimate of cover can be obtained by regular sampling. The area should be sampled with two sets of transects at 90° to correct for bias due to asymmetry of the habitat patches. At 1:10,000 scale it is convenient to use the 1km grid lines for this purpose, taking ten north-south and ten east-west transects in each 10 km square, giving a total scale of length transect of 200 km. This will give a reasonable estimate of cover for all but the scarcest habitats. These should be measured directly. If carried out over all maps in the survey area, or possibly on a carefully stratified representative sample, the method will give a useful estimate of the proportions of each habitat in the area surveyed. The accuracy of the method should be checked against dot grid measurements to give error estimates.

## 3.8 Digitisation

If the equipment is available, a digitising graphics tablet linked to a microcomputer is an effective method of measuring areas on the habitat maps and the resulting data can be readily stored and processed on the computer.

Full digitisation of the maps, on the other hand, is a major undertaking but once completed it allows a wealth of information to be extracted in the minimum of time. The digitisation of all the information on the base maps and the superimposed habitat map is a time-consuming and exacting task but the likely availability of digitised base maps in the future would simplify the procedure considerably, so that the work involved would be little more than that of area measurement.

It should be noted that digitised maps require a very large data storage capacity and that a large colour printer is needed to output habitat maps information. Once digitised, maps can be printed out at any scale and using any frame. This is useful where sites of interest overlap several maps.

The digitised habitat data can of course be used directly for area measurement and subsequent analysis and can also be fed into a GIS (Geographical Information System), which would allow it to be combined by computer with other spatially distributed data for the survey area.

Although the availability of this technology is still very recent, some surveys have been fully digitised. The Cheshire Phase 1 survey made use of the mainframe computing facilities at the county planning office, including a large scale digitiser and plotter, while the Wigan Phase 1 survey used a much smaller PC-based system with a 6-colour A3 plotter. Both systems allow any portion of any map, or maps, to be printed out on request.

## 3.9  Accuracy

Survey results should always be produced with as much accuracy and consistency as time and resources will allow. Ideally, estimates of the probable error should accompany all numerical data on habitat abundance and distribution, but in practice, error estimation is not easy to accomplish and limited resources may be better allocated to minimising the error.

The errors involved in measuring habitat areas on 1:10,000 scale maps are likely in most cases to be well below 5%. A statistical treatment of these errors is not likely to be justified unless a sampling procedure has been used, in which case the standard error resulting from the sampling should be estimated in the usual way.

The greatest source of error is likely to be the 'observer error' in assigning the habitat to one category or another. As there is no absolute method of determining habitat categories in the field, this error can only be estimated by having different trained observers map the same areas in the field. This exercise is well worth carrying out on a limited scale and will also give information on the second most important source of error - the boundary error involved in mapping unbounded habitat units.

Accuracy may be kept high by a number of procedures.

Initial training and subsequent supervision and monitoring of surveyors and cartographers must be thorough.

Selected areas should be surveyed independently by two or more surveyors, and the results compared. Sources of error for any appreciable discrepancies must be identified and corrective procedures initiated.

Experienced Phase 1 surveyors should be brought in from outside to check over randomly selected areas. This will help to ensure consistency at a national level.

If surveyors operate in pairs or small groups, then the members of such pairs or groups should be interchanged on occasion.

From time to time, the edges of survey areas should be overlapped and comparisons made of the mapped areas which coincide.

The identification of dominant species should be checked, possibly by asking surveyors to bring back specimens for confirmation of identification.

Target notes should be reviewed periodically to ensure that they are attaining the agreed minimum standard.

Team leaders should check independently and thoroughly that map information is being transcribed accurately, both from field to fair maps and from fair to master maps. Where cartographers are employed, they must refer problems back to the surveyors.

Habitat areas should be measured independently over a sample of map sheets.

If these procedures are followed, it will be possible to generate estimates of error for each of the following operations:-

classification of habitats in the field;

determination of habitat boundaries;

transcription of mapped information;

measurement of habitat areas.

If doubt exists as to how to calculate statistical limits, a statistician should be consulted. Errors should be presented and discussed in full in the survey report, and the validity of results assessed in view of them.

## 3.10  Interpretation of Phase 1 survey maps

All users of Phase 1 habitat maps should be aware of their limitations. Maps should not be lent or copied without a covering note on their use, otherwise they may do more harm than good. A policy decision should be made as to who will receive the information and how it is to be disseminated. Users should be encouraged to consult NCC regional offices, or those responsible for the Phase 1 survey, about the interpretation of Phase 1 habitat maps.

It is recommended that all habitat maps should be accompanied by a caveat such as this:-

'Although this map has been produced with the intention of indicating and classifying the occurrence of semi-natural habitats, it is not to be regarded as a definitive representation of the conservation value or interest of any piece of land. In particular, the absence of any symbol such as a colour code or target symbol should not be taken as denoting a lack of conservation value.'

The following points must be considered when interpreting habitat maps. Firstly, the maps should not be used as the sole basis of assessing the likely effects of specific land-use change proposals for the following reasons:-

the maps are not 100% accurate, as will be reflected by the error estimates (see 3.9);

many important animal communities will not be indicated because the maps are based on vegetation;

significant habitat changes may have occurred since the maps were produced;

habitats smaller than the specified minimum are not mapped;

sites are visited only once, so some communities may have been missed due to seasonal effects;

no attempt is made to construct complete species lists and rarities may have been overlooked.

Secondly, all mapped habitats are not of equal conservation value, and indeed all sites of any particular habitat type are not of equal value. Thirdly, even if a habitat is widespread, it may still be threatened. The great majority of it may be seriously damaged, leaving only small patches in good condition. Quite large tracts of habitat may only be remnants of more extensive cover and may themselves be vanishing or changing rapidly. The maps give no indication of the rates of change of habitats.

## 3.11 Evaluation

Strictly speaking, site evaluation is not the concern of Phase 1 survey. Nevertheless, because the value of any site depends upon the context within which it is to be evaluated, Phase 1 survey of a large number of sites in the same general area does afford a basis for comparison. Therefore a Phase 1 surveyor is well placed to make such a comparison.

In drawing comparisons, surveyors should make clear the limited nature of the information used in the assessment. Phase 1 survey is rapid and fairly superficial, and the single visit may have been carried out at a less than ideal time of year. Also, the survey is based simply on vegetation and other aspects of wildlife are not considered.

On the basis of Phase 1 survey information alone it is possible to categorise sites on a three-point scale as follows:-

1 site of high conservation priority

2 site of lower priority for conservation

3 site of limited wildlife interest

The principles and criteria used in evaluating wildlife habitats are set out in *A nature conservation review* (Ratcliffe 1977) and *Wildlife conservation evaluation* (Usher 1986). Reference may also be made to *Guidelines for selection of biological SSSIs* (NCC 1989). Evaluation criteria include naturalness, diversity, rarity of species and habitat types, site size and spatial relationships between habitats. Although fragmentation is usually detrimental, mosaics of semi-natural habitats are often of great importance for animal communities. Diversity is not always a good indication of conservation value - for example habitats on acid soils tend to be inherently less diverse than those on neutral or basic soils.

The criteria used for evaluating sites should be made clear and shortcomings, such as the need for further information, pointed out. The nature of the wildlife interest in the three site categories should be explained. Sites should not be ranked within these categories. Although categorisation is necessary, it should be stressed that all semi-natural habitat is of wildlife value and that areas of low intrinsic interest may play a vital role as wildlife corridors and be very important for wide-ranging and dispersed species.

Maps showing suggested site boundaries at a suitable scale (probably 1:25,000) can be provided for areas of conservation interest. Brief site descriptions should be written. Where doubt exists over whether to include a piece of land within the boundary, this should be mentioned, with the reasons.

Where Phase 2 survey might subsequently be undertaken, a different site classification has been found useful. The site categories are:-

1 sites meriting Phase 2 survey

2 sites of wildlife interest which are worth a further visit but do not, at present, merit Phase 2 survey

3 sites of wildlife interest not meriting further survey.

## 3.12 Use of hierarchical alphanumeric habitat codes

The Phase 1 survey habitat classification presented in this manual and summarised in Appendix 1 is a hierarchical system in which each habitat may be represented by an alphanumeric code. These codes are also set out in Appendix 2, which shows the mnemonic lettered codes used in habitat mapping in the field.

The alphanumeric codes have been chosen so as to be consistent with the earlier NCC/RSNC habitat classification (NCC/RSNC 1984) and habitat recording on SSSIs (see Section 9.1). The use of codes alongside the name of a habitat type, for example wet heath (D2), broadleaved semi-natural woodland (A1.1.1), indicates that the habitat has been defined according to the Phase 1 survey system.

It is recommended that the alphanumeric codes are used when listing the habitats present on a given site and in compiling habitat information for computer databases. According to preference and precedent they may also be used on monochrome maps as an alternative to the lettered habitat codes.

# 4 Urban surveys

The Phase 1 classification and survey methodology presented in this manual are directly applicable to urban surveys, with only slight modifications to allow for the larger scale and greater detail which may be required.

## 4.1 Choice of scale

Because of the limited range and extent of wildlife habitats in most urban areas, the significance of relatively small sites is increased. Some sites may be quite complex and intricate and the use of a large map scale allows them to be represented more clearly. The use of very large map scales, such as 1:2500, is only likely to be feasible where the total survey area is quite small. It should be noted that a scale of 1:10,000 has been found suitable for many urban surveys including the surveys of Greater London and West Midlands.

In urban areas, wildlife habitat tends to occur as islands in a sea of urban development, so that it appears to consist of a series of isolated sites. However, as in intensively farmed areas, the relationship between these sites is important and any linear habitats or chains of smaller sites linking one area with another may be of considerable value. It is easier to see these relationships on a 1:10,000 scale map than on a larger scale map, which necessarily encompasses a much smaller area.

The use of a 1:10,000 scale for both urban and rural surveys allows both surveys to be represented on the same map. This allows the relationships between the wildlife habitats in the two areas to be clearly discerned. In practice there is often no clear boundary between urban and rural areas. The transition from one to the other may be gradual and may extend over a considerable distance. Furthermore, county, district and other 'rural' surveys must, of necessity, include many towns and villages, some of which may be quite extensive. Clearly there is a considerable advantage in applying a uniform methodology over the whole area.

The availability of reasonably up-to-date cartography is a further point in favour of the use of a 1:10,000 scale, because in many urban areas the larger scale maps are long out of date.

## 4.2 Target notes

The relative importance of small sites and the frequent occurrence of complex habitat mosaics in urban areas leads to an increased need for descriptive target notes, so it is likely that most sites will require a target note. In many cases this note may be quite brief but it should give an indication of the significance of the site. Indications of past management are at least as important as in rural areas and information on the present ownership should be included where available.

## 4.3 Habitat classification

The habitat classification presented here takes into account the experience of urban surveys such as the Greater London and the St Helens and Knowsley surveys (Game 1984, Ash & Gately 1984) in using earlier versions of the Phase 1 classification. The definitions of several habitats have been expanded and made more rigorous in the light of this experience, in particular the tall ruderal (C3.1) and ephemeral/short perennial (J1.3) habitat classes, which now encompass all early successional communities on derelict land.

Two new categories were added to the original Phase 1 habitat classification in 1986 in response to the needs of urban surveys. These are amenity grassland (J1.2) and introduced shrub (J1.4). Amenity grassland is the prevalent form of open land use in many towns and cities and is readily distinguished from other types of improved or reseeded grassland. Although usually of little value as wildlife habitat, amenity grassland is a major constituent of urban greenspace and a knowledge of its extent and distribution is of importance to nature conservation planning in urban areas. It is worth pointing out that less rigorous mowing regimes and more sympathetic management of at least the margins of amenity grassland could benefit both the amenity and the nature conservation value of such land. The large extent of amenity grassland, clearly visible on urban habitat maps, often contrasts markedly with the much smaller areas of semi-natural habitat, making clear the need to conserve the latter.

It should be stressed that the amenity grassland category (J1.2) applies only to closely mown amenity grassland. Other forms of amenity land and other habitats occurring within amenity grasslands should be mapped according to their vegetation as woodland, heathland, semi-improved grassland, etc.

The introduced shrub category (J1.4) is regarded as sufficiently distinct to warrant a class of its own and should be used for large stands of non-native shrubs, whether single-species or multi-species stands, and for mixed stands where non-native species predominate over native shrubs. Where native shrubs predominate, the stand should be mapped as scrub (A2) and the non-native species target noted. Introduced tall herbs, such as *Reynoutria japonica* should be mapped as tall ruderal (C3.1).

## 4.4 Survey procedure

Much of the methodology described in previous sections is equally applicable to urban survey. The purpose of this section is to draw attention to some of the techniques and procedures which have been used to deal with the particular problems arising in urban surveys.

One of the first problems after deciding on the scope and scale of the survey is to locate the areas of wildlife habitat requiring field survey - the 'wildlife sites'. The usefulness of aerial photography for this task has already been noted (see Section 2.2) but it must be up-to-date. Ordnance Survey maps are seldom fully up-to-date; many are more than 10 years old, some rely heavily on earlier surveys, and even the latest editions cannot incorporate the most recent developments in the urban landscape. Whereas recent maps and aerial photography are useful in planning the survey, they are no substitute for direct field survey as a means of locating, defining and describing wildlife sites.

The use of a car, essential in rural surveys, is generally more of a hindrance than a help in urban areas and the survey is best carried out on foot, bicycle or public transport. Bicycles have been found to be very useful in many urban surveys and provide a means of covering considerable distances while still allowing the surveyor to stop and investigate at will.

Survey on foot will generally need to be combined with use of public transport and advantage should be taken of this opportunity to obtain a view of other areas in the neighbourhood from bus or train. Suburban trains were found to be particularly useful in the Greater London survey, providing a view of the railside habitats and of other habitats in the vicinity of the railway.

Although many urban wildlife sites have open access, some will require access to be negotiated in advance and may be either in public or private ownership. Casual local enquiries by the surveyor may provide the necessary information on ownership and also on the past history of the site. Failing this, enquiry should be made of the local wildlife trust, the Nature Conservancy Council or the local council planning department.

Contact with the public in the course of urban survey is unavoidable and can be beneficial to both sides, but needs to be prepared for. Many members of the public will be curious about the activities of the Phase 1 surveyor and some may be interested in the aims and objectives of the survey.

Some members of the public may be able to provide useful information which will increase the value of the survey or facilitate the work of the surveyor. Others may wish to ask for advice on habitat management. Clearly, talking to the public during the course of a survey can be an opportunity to promote the ideas and objectives of nature conservation and may be of direct benefit to the survey. However, the surveyor has a responsibility to maintain the pace of the survey and will usually need to limit contact with the public to the minimum, referring enquiries to others for more detailed or more definite responses.

In the same way, because of the greater populations in urban areas and the time needed to deal with large numbers of responses or enquiries, careful thought will need to be given to the amount of publicity to be given to the survey and, in particular, to whether to make an appeal for information or simply to survey the area 'on sight'.

It should be clearly understood that Phase 1 survey is essentially a reconnaissance survey to establish the nature, extent and distribution of the wildlife habitat resource. In urban surveys, as in other areas, the surveyor should guard against being led by the scarcity of the habitat or the complexity of the site into attempting to survey in greater detail than is required or justified at Phase 1.

If more detailed survey is required, it may be most efficient to carry out Phase 2 survey at the same time as Phase 1, but this requirement needs to be clearly recognised and resourced from the outset.

## 4.5 Phase 2 survey

The need for more detailed information on practically all wildlife habitat sites in urban areas results in the need for Phase 2 survey to cover virtually the full extent of the Phase 1 survey, in terms of both the number of sites and the range of habitats. This is markedly different from the situation in rural surveys where Phase 2 survey is commonly restricted to a single habitat type, such as woodland or grassland, and to a limited number of sites within this category, the sites being selected from the completed Phase 1 survey.

Urban Phase 2 survey is therefore usually a relatively comprehensive multi-habitat survey and may be carried out either concurrently with the Phase 1 survey or as a follow-up after completion of Phase 1. Most, though not all, urban surveys have found it convenient to carry out Phase 2 survey at the same time as Phase 1.

Up to the present, most urban Phase 2 surveys have been based on *A Conspectus of urban vegetation types* devised by Shimwell (1983). This describes and classifies some 160 different plant communities of urban habitats, but some users have found it necessary to add to this list. The National Vegetation Classification (Rodwell in prep.) will probably supersede the Shimwell classification. These systems are too detailed for Phase 1 survey and should not be used for this purpose, although the Shimwell classification fits the Phase 1 classification quite well. Ideally, separate Phase 1 and Phase 2 maps should be produced, possibly at different scales. The Phase 1 target notes should be expanded to include reference to the Phase 2 information, which will probably be stored separately.

The value of Phase 1 survey should not be overlooked, even where a comprehensive Phase 2 survey is carried out. The Phase 1 survey provides a concise overview of the whole survey area and its relative simplicity is particularly useful for strategic conservation planning, for overall resource evaluation and for monitoring habitat change.

Table 7 shows the resources needed for combined Phase 1 and Phase 2 surveys in three urban areas.

Table 7  Some figures on urban survey rates

| Survey | Map scale | Approx area within survey boundary (km$^2$) | Approx number of 'sites' surveyed | Number of surveyors employed | Approx area covered by surveyor per day (km$^2$) | Time taken to complete survey |
|---|---|---|---|---|---|---|
| West Midlands CC | 1:10,000 | 880 | 20,000 'habitat parcels' | 4 | 4 | 1 year (2 days per week in field) |
| GLC/LWT Greater London | 1:10,000 | 1580 | 1900 sites | 5-6 | 3-4 | 9 months |
| Groundwork Trust St Helens & Knowsley | 1:2,500 | 60 | 80 sites worth Phase 2 survey/target notes | 2 | 1 | 5 months (part-time) |

# 5 Using the colour code mapping system

## 5.1 Use of colour

It is strongly recommended that the final habitat maps should be colour-coded (see Appendix 1). The use of colour allows complex situations to be presented clearly and enables a rapid visual assessment to be made of the abundance and distribution of particular habitats.

Coloured maps may be duplicated by making full-colour photocopies or, if large numbers are required, it may be preferable to make a monochrome copy by tracing onto acetate sheet and photocopying this in the normal way. Alternatively, where monochrome maps have been produced using alphanumeric or mnemonic lettered codes, one or two copies should be coloured in for use by those most likely to consult the habitat maps frequently, whilst the other monochrome copies may be used as they stand, or coloured in by their users.

Only the standard Berol Verithin colour pencils specified in Appendix 1 should be used. Colour should be applied with a moderate pressure and shading kept even so as not to obscure underlying detail on the printed map. Colours will photocopy best if shading is even and not too light.

Hatched lines should be spaced 2.5 to 5 mm apart, depending on the size of the habitat unit, and should be at 45° to the vertical except where the shape and orientation of the habitat unit makes it preferable to vary this. Cross-hatching lines should intersect at 90°. The use of a Linex hatching apparatus is helpful in producing accurately spaced hatching, otherwise a set square and ruler (or T-square) should be used. The direction of hatching shown for each habitat in the coloured key in Part 2 should be adhered to.

Where there is no marked boundary between habitats a dashed line in black ink (0.35 mm) should be marked in. This greatly facilitates visual assessment of the map and subsequent area measurement.

The minimum mappable area at 1:10,000 scale is about 0.1 ha for solid colour and 0.25 ha for hatching. (At 1:25,000 scale the equivalent areas are 0.5 ha and 1.5 ha respectively). Areas of interest smaller than this should be marked with a target symbol and described in a target note (see Section 6).

Linear areas less than 25 m wide should be represented by a single line of the appropriate colour, and should be marked with a target symbol and described in a target note if of interest. Linear habitats such as marginal vegetation, strandline vegetation, hedges, ditches and roadside verges will always need to be treated in this way.

When mapping acid grassland in hilly areas, confusion with calcareous grassland may arise owing to the intersection of the orange hatching with brown contour lines. This problem may be alleviated by drawing the lines for acid grassland routinely at 5 mm spacing and calcareous grassland at 2.5 mm spacing.

## 5.2 Additional codes

The colour codes for scattered scrub, scattered trees and scattered bracken are designed to be superimposed on the appropriate code for the underlying vegetation, and combined codes are specified for mosaics of acid grassland with wet heath and dry heath, but in general, transitional and mixed habitats should be represented by the code for the most prevalent habitat and the relative proportions of the other habitats recorded in a target note. In cases where a new combination is necessary this should be shown in a key attached to the habitat map.

In a given survey it may be considered desirable to drop the use of certain codes under specific circumstances, for example the code for unvegetated crags might be dropped where these are numerous and evident from the Ordnance Survey symbols. Likewise, as previously noted, a decision may be made not to map hedges and walls. These departures from the standard should be noted in the key.

The habitat coding system has been widely used over a number of years in many different parts of the country and it should not be necessary to devise new habitat codes. If the need for additional codes does arise, it is recommended that the England Headquarters, Nature Conservancy Council, Peterborough, should be consulted on their use. Any new codes agreed on must not conflict in any way with existing codes and should be shown in a key on the habitat map.

# 6 Target notes

## 6.1 Importance of target notes

Target notes are an essential part of Phase 1 survey and increase considerably the value of the habitat maps by providing:–

supplementary information on sites of interest (for example species composition, structure and management);

information on sites too small to map and on sites where habitat mapping is found to be difficult or doubtful (for example transitional and mixed habitats);

information on sites previously surveyed and sites requiring further survey.

The more numerous and more detailed the target notes are, the more useful the survey will be. A target note should enable others to make a preliminary assessment of the nature conservation value of a given site and a comparison between one site and another. It is likely that the target notes will form the chief basis of site selection for conservation planning and for further survey at Phase 2 level.

Before starting a survey, careful consideration should be given to deciding which habitats and which types of site are to be target noted. The decisions made must be followed thereafter, so that a consistent and workable set of target notes is produced. Such factors as the skill and training of the surveyors and the prevalence and importance of particular habitats must be taken into account. However, the most important consideration will be the resources available, because making target notes is a time-consuming process.

## 6.2 Target note content

The overall aim of the target note is to give a succinct picture of the nature conservation interest of a site in the context of its land-use and management.

Target notes must be clear, concise and informative. Even the briefest of descriptions, for example 'ancient coppiced sessile oak/birch woodland with hazel understorey and acid ground flora', can greatly enhance the value of the habitat map.

Ideally, each discrete unit of semi-natural vegetation should be target noted, but in practice small and uninteresting areas are usually omitted in order to maintain the speed of the survey.. If necessary, note that a site was not visited or needs a further visit. It is important to target note sites in which wildlife interest has been reduced or destroyed.

The following should always be included in the target note:–

habitat type or types present together with their dominant plant species;

other species of note;

need for further survey if relevant;

Where time and resources allow, the following elements may also be included:–

a description of the habitat structure, topography and substrate;

a description of the plant communities present;

details of any noteworthy animal associations;

a note of any known rare species of plant or animal;

notes on past, present or proposed management practices;

details of ownership (if found in passing);

details of any form of site protection;

notes on any changes, particularly if damaging, that have occurred recently, or are taking place, or are threatened;

reference to, or results of, any previous surveys;

A list of key words, such as that given in Appendix 4, is helpful in the preparation and computerisation of target notes.

## 6.3 Target note format

The site to be target noted is marked on the map with a red target symbol. The full grid reference for this point is recorded in the target note, together with the date of survey (month and year) and the initials of the surveyors.

Grid references estimated in the field must be checked and all grid references measured on the finished map with a Romer grid or a metric scale, to ensure that they are correct.

The site name, if any, should be given, followed

by information as detailed in section 6.2. Information from previous surveys should be given in the standard target note form, with original date and surveyors, and source.

Botanical nomenclature should follow the *Excursion flora of the British Isles*, 3rd Edition (Clapham *et al.* 1981) or the *Flora of the British Isles*, 3rd edition (Clapham *et al.* 1987). Vernacular names may be used in the habitat descriptions (for example 'ash-hazel woodland with holly'), provided ambiguity is avoided (for example specify 'sessile oak', or 'oak (*Q. petraea*)' rather than just 'oak'). Systematic names of species should be given in full and are particularly important when noting rare species.

Target notes may be typed in numerical order of their grid references on A4 sheets, with the notes for each 1 km square starting on a fresh page, identified by the 4-figure grid reference for the square. Alternatively, the notes may be typed individually on reference cards. This system facilitates up-dating, but is cumbersome to store and tedious to manage, as a county survey may generate several thousand target notes. A typical page of target notes is shown in Appendix 5.

The target note symbols on the habitat maps may be numbered sequentially in grid reference order, but this is not essential, since the grid reference should be sufficient to locate the target symbol.

The informal descriptive target note is readable and gives an impression of the site as perceived by the surveyor, but covers only those features considered to be significant. This degree of subjectivity and selectivity is a weakness if what is required is a consistent, objective record of an agreed set of characteristics for each site. The creation of a computer database favours a more structured form of target note and to this end it is suggested that a standard form, such as that shown in Appendix 6, is used for target note recording. The use of such a form will help to standardise the information noted by the surveyor and to avoid the omission of potentially important information due to oversight, while still allowing a descriptive account to be written. Some repetitive information, such as vice-county and local authority district, can be filled in before photocopying the relevant batches of forms for use by the surveyors.

## 6.4 General descriptions

A useful addition to the set of target notes for each 5 km or 10 km square is a concise general description of the geology, topography and nature conservation interest of that square. This introduction to the habitat map and target notes for the given square is particularly useful to persons unfamiliar with the area and should be filed at the beginning of the relevant set of target notes.

The general description sheets also provide a useful resource on which to base district and county reports.

# 7 Data storage

## 7.1 Survey products

The products resulting from Phase 1 survey are:-

a series of habitat maps;

a set of habitat area measurements and statistics;

a file of target notes;

a survey report, including resource statement and overview.

These products are likely to have a working life of at least 10 years and must be stored securely. On the other hand the survey results are likely to be most useful and most used if they are readily accessible. Storage facilities must meet these two requirements - security and accessibility.

## 7.2 Habitat maps

Completed habitat maps should be mounted and stored, in grid-reference order, in vertical-hanging steel map cabinets. A3 size photocopies may be stored flat in drawers, folded to A4 and filed or hung vertically.

Field maps should be retained and are most conveniently stored by folding to A4 size and filing in grid square order in storage files.

For security purposes a duplicate set of maps should be kept at a separate location. These may be in the form of coloured fair copies, colour photocopies, 35 mm colour transparencies mounted as slides or microfiches, or fully coded monochrome maps. This copy set may be held by another organisation, provided it is accessible in an emergency.

Fully digitised habitat maps are, of course, stored on tape or disk in the computer system, but the paper originals must also be stored carefully in case of loss or damage to these data.

## 7.3 Habitat area data

Habitat area measurements should be stored on paper, filed in grid square order in storage files. Where computing facilities are available they should be input onto a computer data-file and stored on tape or disk with a back-up copy. A standard form for use in computerising map sheet data is given in Appendix 6.

## 7.4 Target notes

Completed target notes and general description sheets should be filed in grid square order in a metal filing cabinet. A duplicate set should be stored at a separate location. This requirement is met if a related organisation has a full duplicate set.

There are considerable advantages to be gained from storing target note information on a computer database. Large quantities of target notes may be stored in this way in a very compact and easily accessible form. They can be updated readily and the information in them can be selected, sorted and printed out in any form. For ease of reference, target notes are best stored on a PC-based system and a number of systems have been developed for this purpose, using commercially available software. Thus, Cheshire County Council has developed a Heritage Database package using PC-PROMISE from Duncan Databases (Ramsay 1985) and Wigan Borough Council uses DATA-EASE from Honeywell (Wigan MBC 1987).

NCC is currently developing a standardised package for recording Phase 1 survey data. It is intended that this package will be compatible with the COREDATA system used by NCC for recording information on statutory sites and with RECORDER (Ball 1988), which is used in local biological records centres.

The standard target note recording form shown in Appendix 6 will probably be adopted for use with the NCC Phase 1 survey database, and can be used in the field.

# 8 The survey report

The final task of the survey, after the habitat maps, target notes and habitat area measurements are completed, is to produce the survey report. This is a very important element of the survey and adequate time and resources must be allocated to it.

The purpose of the report is to present the results of the survey in a concise form to the potential user, summarising and interpreting them so as to facilitate their use in conservation planning. The report should give an overview of the wildlife habitat resource of the survey area in terms of quantitative data, with interpretation and comment, supported by a descriptive account of the resource.

Ideally, a separate report should be produced for each local authority district and a further report for the whole county. Where districts are small, a single county report will suffice but separate habitat statistics should be produced for each district.

The time taken to write and produce a report varies considerably with the amount of detail required and with the experience of the participants but it is a valuable exercise for all concerned, providing an opportunity for the surveyors to take a broader view of their work and to present their accumulated experience to others. The task may be divided between the surveyors by habitat or by district, the former being probably the most satisfactory. The work involved in editing the text and producing maps, diagrams and tables should not be underestimated and 10-12 man-weeks would not be too much time to allocate to the writing and production of a report.

The report must describe how the survey was carried out, as this may have a bearing on the interpretation of the results, and should indicate briefly the nature of the area to be surveyed. It should present a summary of the habitat area statistics in the form of tables, pie-charts and distribution maps. These collectively constitute a quantitative resource statement for the county or district (see Kelly & Perry 1990; NCC 1983a, b, 1986a). This is expanded and interpreted in the descriptive section, which should include for each habitat type in the survey area, a description of its character, distribution and importance and an indication of current and threatened changes. The report should draw attention to typical and outstanding examples of particular habitats in the survey area and to important sites and aggregations of sites but it is not necessarily the role of the surveyor to evaluate these or to make recommendations as to action. The purpose of the survey is to provide sufficient information to enable others to evaluate sites and to decide upon appropriate action. If evaluation is required, refer to section 3.11.

The report should be designed to be read by environmental planners as well as by ecologists and nature conservation specialists. To this end it is recommended that English names of flowering plants should be included, together with their Latin systematic names. English names should follow the nomenclature of Dony *et al.* (1986), which should be quoted as a reference. Where a local variant of the English names is preferred the standarised English name should be labelled in brackets.

The report should include full references to previous surveys and other sources of information incorporated into the survey in the form of target notes.

A copy of the report should be sent to the England Headquarters, Nature Conservancy Council, Peterborough.

# 9 Comparison of Phase 1 survey classification with other classifications

## 9.1 The SSSI habitat mapping scheme and the NCC/RSNC classification

Appendix 7 shows the habitat classification agreed between NCC and the Royal Society for Nature Conservation (NCC/RSNC1984). This scheme is very similar to the system used by NCC to map SSSIs (NCC 1982). The differences between the two are indicated in Appendix 7.

The revised Phase 1 habitat classification (Appendix 1) differs from the SSSI and NCC/RSNC systems in a number of details, but there is one major difference: for Phase 1 there are four mire categories – bog, flush and spring, fen, bare peat – rather than two. Less importantly, in the revised Phase 1 classification single-species dominant swamp and tall fen vegetation are combined in a single swamp category; fore, yellow and grey dunes are combined as open dune, and coastal lagoons are classified as brackish standing water, rather than being included in coastal habitats (J).

Habitat categories which are now used for Phase 1 survey, but are not included in either the SSSI habitat mapping scheme or the NCC/RSNC classification, are:

| | | |
|---|---|---|
| Parkland/scattered trees | - | broad-leaved |
| | - | coniferous |
| | - | mixed |
| Recently-felled woodland | - | broad-leaved |
| | - | coniferous |
| | - | mixed |

Poor semi-improved grassland
Fen
Flood-plain mire
Refuse-tip
Cultivated/

| | | |
|---|---|---|
| disturbed ground | - | arable |
| | - | amenity grassland |
| | - | ephemeral/short perennial |
| | - | introduced shrub |
| Hedges | - | native species-rich |
| | - | species-poor |

Earth bank
Sea wall

All instances where the classification and corresponding alphanumeric reference codes for Phase 1 survey differ from those used in the SSSI or NCC/RSNC systems are indicated in Appendix 1 by an asterisk. All new categories in the Phase 1 system have been given unique alphanumeric codes, to avoid confusion with previously used codes. The gaps in the numbering system correspond to codes in the SSSI and NCC/RSNC classifications which are not used in the Phase 1 system. The alternative series of lettered habitat codes (Appendix 2) is unique to the Phase 1 system.

The coloured symbols (hatching patterns, overlaid letters, etc) used in the SSSI habitat mapping system differ in a number of ways from those used for Phase 1 habitat mapping. However, the colours themselves are the same in both systems for all the major habitat types except fen.

## 9.2 The Draft Phase 1 habitat mapping manual

The habitat classification, alphanumeric codes and lettered habitat codes in the draft *Habitat mapping manual (Phase 1)* (NCC 1986b), differ a little from the revised version presented in Appendices 1 and 2 and Part 2 of this manual.

The changes that have been made to the categories and alphanumeric codes are given in Table 8.

### Table 8

| | Draft version | Final version |
|---|---|---|
| Mixed parkland/scattered trees | - | A3.3 |
| Mixed recently-felled woodland | - | A4.3 |
| Poor semi-improved grassland | - | B6 |
| Fen | - | E3 |
| Valley mire | E1.10 | E3.1 |
| Basin mire | E1.9 | E3.2 |
| Flood-plain mire | - | E3.3 |
| Bare peat | E1.11 | E4 |
| Swamp - single species dom. | F1.1 | ) Combined as |
| - tall | F1.2 | ) F1 (swamp) |
| Dystrophic running water | - | G2.4 |
| Fore dune | H6.1 | ) Combined as |
| Yellow dune | H6.2 | ) H6.8 |
| Grey dune | H6.3 | ) (open dune) |
| Cliff crevice/ledge vegetation | H8.6 | H8.3 |
| Natural rock - other acid | I1.8 | I1.4.1 (acid/neutral) |
| - other basic | I1.9 | I1.4.2 |
| Ditch - permanently wet | J2.6.1 | Included in G1 |
| - seasonally wet | J2.6.2 | J2.6 (dry ditch) |

The colour codings in the revision remain the same as in the draft manual, except that solid sky blue now denotes both single-species dominant and tall swamp, as these categories have been merged. Changes that have been made to the original lettered habitat codes are given in Table 9.

### Table 9

| | Draft version | Final version |
|---|---|---|
| Parkland/scattered trees - broadleaved | BP | SBW |
| - coniferous | CP | SCW |
| - mixed | - | SMW |
| Mixed recently-felled woodland | - | FM |
| Poor semi-improved grassland | - | SI |
| Flood-plain mire | - | FPM |
| Swamp - single-species dominant | SD | ) SP |
| - tall | TS | ) |
| Standing open water - eutrophic | E | SWE |
| - mesotrophic | M | SWM |
| - oligotrophic | O | SWO |
| - dystrophic | D | SWD |
| - marl | C | SWC |
| - brackish | B | SWB |
| Running open water - eutrophic | E | RWE |
| - mesotrophic | M | RWM |
| - oligotrophic | O | RWO |
| - dystrophic | - | RWD |
| - marl | C | RWC |
| - brackish | B | RWB |

| | | |
|---|---|---|
| Saltmarsh - dense/continuous | DSm | DSM |
| - scattered plants | SSm | SSM |
| Sand dune - fore dune | FD | ) |
| - yellow dune | YD | ) OD |
| - grey dune | GD | ) |
| Rock exposure and waste - cave | Ca | CA |
| - mine | Mi | MI |
| Intact hedge - native species-rich | H | RH |
| - species-poor | H | H |
| Defunct hedge - native species-rich | H- | RH- |
| - species-poor | H- | H- |
| Hedge and trees - native species-rich | HT | RHT |
| - species-poor | HT | HT |
| Dry ditch | D | DD |

The Royal Society for the Protection of Birds has issued a manual (Evans 1988) for use in habitat classification and recording on their reserves.

This is a modified version of the 1986 draft Phase 1 habitat mapping manual.

## 9.3 The National Vegetation Classification (NVC)

The habitat classification used for Phase 1 survey is a broad one, although further subdivided by species coding, and reflects the conservation interest of the habitats. Thus, woodlands and grasslands are subdivided into various categories but arable land is not.

The habitat categories are defined in Part 2 of this manual and the relationships between these categories and the community types of the National Vegetation Classification (Rodwell in prep.) are shown in Appendix 8. In general there is no one-to-one correspondence between the two systems. Each habitat type may include a number of different NVC community types and, in some cases, the same NVC community may occur in several different habitat types. This is an unavoidable consequence of the fact that the two systems are based on different approaches to the classification of vegetation.

Although the NVC system is much too detailed for use in Phase 1 surveys it is now standard for Phase 2 surveys, so it may be useful for surveyors to be aware of the relationship between the NVC and the Phase 1 classification.

Further information on the NVC communities of different habitats is to be found in *Guidelines for selection of biological SSSIs* (NCC 1989).

# Part 2
# Field manual

# 1 Habitat classification and coding

As explained in Part 1, habitats may be mapped using colour codes (Appendix 1), a hierarchical alphanumeric coding system, or lettered codes (Appendix 2).

The full range of the classification should be used wherever possible, although this may at times prove difficult. For example, it may be impossible to determine the trophic status of a water body or to tell whether a fen is a basin, valley or flood-plain mire. For this reason the recording of some habitat types is optional, as indicated in Appendix 1. In cases such as dry heath/acid grassland, the existence of vegetation mosaics has been recognised and a combination of colours is used in mapping.

The use of codes for dominant species (Appendix 3) effectively provides a further subdivision of the habitat categories and is recommended for use wherever practicable. Target notes give additional detail and they can also be used to clarify areas of difficulty in categorisation or mapping. Key words for use in compiling target notes are given in Appendix 4. A number of examples of target notes and a standard target note recording form are given in Appendices 5 and 6.

**Part 1 of this manual should be read before any fieldwork is undertaken.**

# 2 Habitat definitions

This section provides definitions for each of the habitats which have been distinguished for the purpose of Phase 1 survey. The definitions given are based on those used by the NCC for surveying SSSIs (see Appendix 7). Appendix 8 shows the National Vegetation Classification (NVC) communities to be expected in each Phase 1 habitat category.

## A   Woodland and scrub

### A1   Woodland

Woodland is defined as vegetation dominated by trees more than 5m high when mature, forming a distinct, although sometimes open, canopy. Dominant species should be coded and the understorey and ground layer target noted. Distinct blocks of woodland, whether broadleaved or coniferous, should be mapped separately wherever possible.

The definitions of the main categories are:-

broadleaved woodland: 10% or less conifer in the canopy;

coniferous woodland: 10% or less broadleaved in the canopy;

mixed woodland: 10-90% of either broadleaved or conifer in the canopy. The approximate proportions of the two types should be target noted.

If the cover of trees is less than 30% the area should be shown as scattered trees on the appropriate background colour. Where the cover is higher than 30% but there are sizeable open spaces or rides, these should be target noted to describe the ground flora.

### Semi-natural woodland

Semi-natural woodland comprises all stands which do not obviously originate from planting. The distribution of species will generally reflect natural variations in the site and its soil. Both ancient and more recent stands are included. Woodland with both semi-natural and planted trees should be classified as semi-natural if the planted trees account for less than 30% of the canopy composition, but as plantation if more than 30% is planted. In cases where it is doubtful whether or not a wood should be classified as semi-natural, target notes giving details of origin and species composition are essential. For details of ancient woodland sites see Kirby et al. (1984).

The following should, amongst others, be included in the semi-natural category:-

woods with planted standards in semi-natural coppice;

mature plantations (more than about 120 years old) of native species growing on sites where those species are native and where there are semi-natural woodland ground flora and shrub communities;

self-sown secondary stands of exotic species (for example sycamore, pine on southern heaths, holm oak on Isle of Wight);

alder carr, and willow carr where the willows are more than 5m tall (although *Salix cinerea* should always be classified as scrub);

well-established sweet-chestnut coppice (that is, over 25 years old);

woods which have been completely underplanted, but where the planted trees do not yet contribute to the canopy;

stands of young trees or coppice regrowth, even when less than 5 m.

### Plantation woodland

All obviously planted woodland of any age should be included in this category, with the exception of those types mentioned previously. Orchards should be mapped by placing green hatching over the OS symbols (which should be added where missing), and target notes made giving tree species and details of any conservation interest. Ornamental tree gardens and arboreta should be included here, and target noted where necessary.

### A2   Scrub

Scrub is seral or climax vegetation dominated by locally native shrubs, usually less than 5 m tall, occasionally with a few scattered trees. Dominant species should always be coded. The ground flora under scattered scrub should be coded or target noted.

The following should, amongst others, be included in this category:-

*Ulex europaeus*, *Cytisus scoparius* and *Juniperus communis* scrub;

stands of *Rubus fruticosus* and *Rosa canina*

montane scrub with *Salix lapponum, S. lanata, S. myrsinites, S. arbuscula* or *S. phylicifolia;*

stands of mature *Crataegus monogyna, Prunus spinosa* or *Salix cinerea,* even if more than 5 m tall;

all willow carr less than 5 m tall; all *Salix cinerea* carr;

stands of *Myrica gale* more than 1.5 m tall.

The following should not be included in this category:-

very low *Salix herbacea* (see heathland, D), *Salix repens* (see dune slack, H6.4), or *Myrica gale* (see mire, E);

*Ulex gallii* or *Ulex minor* (see heathland D);

hedges (see J2);

stands of young trees or stump regrowth less than 5 m high, where these represent more than 50% of the immature canopy cover;

stands of introduced shrub species (see J1.4);

scrub on dunes (see H6.7).

## A3    Parkland and scattered trees

Tree cover must be less than 30% to warrant inclusion in this category. For scattered trees over pasture (as in parkland), or over heath, bog, limestone pavement, etc, the green dot symbol should be superimposed on the appropriate habitat colour. The density of dots should be varied in proportion to the density of trees. Dominant species should be coded. Exotic trees should be target noted. Lines of trees forming windbreaks or avenues should be marked as a series of dots with the dominant species code.

## A4    Recently-felled woodland

The only areas of felled trees which should be included in this category are those whose future land use is uncertain, for instance when it is not clear whether they are to be replanted or used for crops. The dominant species which have been felled should be coded and the codes placed in parentheses.

## B    Grassland and marsh

This category includes both areas of herbaceous vegetation dominated by grasses and certain wet communities dominated by *Juncus* species, *Carex* species, *Filipendula ulmaria* or by other marsh herbs. For grasslands where there is a greater than 25% cover of dwarf shrub heaths see heathland (D), for emergent stands of tall reed-grasses see swamp (F1), for coastal grasslands see saltmarsh (H2), dune (H6) and maritime cliff and slope (H8).

Most grasslands have been subjected to some degree of agricultural improvement by repeated grazing, mowing, fertilising, drainage or herbicide treatment. It is important to try to distinguish unimproved and semi-improved from improved grasslands. However, these grassland types form a continuum, so that it is not possible to define each with precision, especially as species critical for their definition are often only observable for a short season in the year. Agricultural improvement usually results in a decrease in the floristic diversity of the sward and dominance by a few quick-growing grasses such as *Lolium perenne, Holcus lanatus* and *Festuca rubra.* The resulting sward composition is likely to vary with intensity of treatment and with the composition of the original sward, so careful field training is necessary to define and maintain the boundaries between these categories. However, residual difficulties are bound to occur.

Grassy roadside verges, railway cuttings and embankments may be very important features, especially in intensively farmed areas. If they are wide enough they should be mapped as the appropriate grassland habitat. Narrow herb-rich verges should be shown by a broken orange line and target noted, if time permits. See also amenity grassland (J1.2).

### Unimproved grassland

Unimproved grasslands are likely to be rare, especially in the lowlands. They may be rank and neglected, mown or grazed. They may have been treated with low levels of farmyard manure, but should not have had sufficient applications of fertiliser or herbicide, or have been so intensively grazed or drained, as to alter the sward composition significantly. Species diversity is often high, with species characteristic of the area and the soils and with a very low percentage of agricultural species.

In cases of doubt, map as semi-improved and target note the need for further information.

### Semi-improved grassland

Semi-improved grassland is a transition category made up of grasslands which have been modified by artificial fertilisers, slurry, intensive grazing, herbicides or drainage, and consequently have a range of species which is less diverse and natural than unimproved grasslands. Such grasslands are still of some conservation value. Semi-improved grassland may originate from partial improvement of acid, neutral or calcareous grassland and should be mapped as such. However, it should be noted that improvement reduces the acid or calcareous character of the grassland, so that this is not always easy to distinguish in the field.

Species diversity will generally be lower than in unimproved grassland in the same area. If the signs of improvement listed under B4 are lacking, the grassland is likely to be semi-improved and should be mapped accordingly. Target notes should be made in all of the better quality sites. Surveyors should be aware of the species compositions indicative of semi-improved conditions in the locality of the survey. See also poor semi-improved grassland (B6).

## B1  Acid grassland

Grassland in this category is often unenclosed, as on hill-grazing land, and occurs on a range of acid soils (pH less than 5.5). It is generally species-poor, and often grades into wet or dry dwarf shrub heath, although it must always have less than 25% dwarf shrub cover (see heathland, especially D5 and D6). Pioneer annual-rich calcifuge communities on dry sandy soils are included in this category, as are wet acidic grasslands typified by species such as *Juncus squarrosus* (but see marsh/marshy grassland, B5).

The following are indicative of acidic conditions when frequent or abundant: *Deschampsia flexuosa*, *Nardus stricta*, *Juncus squarrosus*, *Galium saxatile*, and *Rumex acetosella*.

## B2  Neutral grassland

Typically enclosed and usually more intensively managed than acid or calcareous grassland (except on roadside verges), this category encompasses a wide range of communities occurring on neutral soils (pH 5.5-7.0).

The following are indicative of neutral conditions when frequent or abundant: *Alopecurus pratensis*, *Arrhenatherum elatius*, *Cynosurus cristatus*, *Dactylis glomerata*, *Deschampsia cespitosa*, *Festuca arundinacea* and *Festuca pratensis*. *Lolium perenne* may be present, but when abundant it is indicative of improved grassland (see B4).

Hay meadows will usually fall within this category. Surveyors should be aware that after cutting, a hay meadow can have the appearance of improved pasture as the new growth comes through.

Included in neutral grassland is a range of grasslands which are inundated periodically, permanently moist, or even water-logged (but see marsh/marshy grassland, B5). Examples are:-

> inundated grassland with abundant *Glyceria* species, *Alopecurus geniculatus*, *Poa trivialis* and *Polygonum hydropiper*;

> water meadows and alluvial meadows;

> species-poor *Deschampsia cespitosa* grasslands and grazed *Juncus effusus/Juncus inflexus* - *Holcus lanatus/Deschampsia cespitosa* grasslands;

wet meadows or pastures where grasses are dominant in the sward (cf. marsh/marshy grassland, B5) but with species such as *Caltha palustris*, *Filipendula ulmaria*, *Valeriana* species, *Juncus* species or *Crepis paludosa* present.

## B3  Calcareous grassland

These grasslands are often unenclosed, not managed intensively, and occur on calcareous soils (pH above 7.0). *Dryas octopetala* communities are included. Where the grass is tall, the dominant species is usually either *Brachypodium pinnatum* or *Bromus erectus*, whilst species indicative of short, close-grazed and species-rich calcareous turf are *Koeleria macrantha*, *Avenula pratensis*, *Sesleria albicans*, *Helianthemum nummularium*, *Sanguisorba minor* and *Thymus praecox*.

## B4  Improved grassland

Improved grasslands are those meadows and pastures which have been so affected by heavy grazing, drainage, or the application of herbicides, inorganic fertilisers, slurry or high doses or manure that they have lost many of the species which one could expect to find in an unimproved sward. They have only a very limited range of grasses and a few common forbs, mainly those demanding of nutrients and resistant to grazing. *Lolium perenne*, *Cynosurus cristatus*, *Trifolium repens*, *Rumex acetosa*, *Taraxacum officinale*, *Bellis perennis*, *Ranunculus acris* and *Ranunculus bulbosus* are typical of improved grassland, while stands of dock *Rumex* species, common nettle *Urtica dioica* and thistles *Cirsium* species indicate local enrichment of the soil by grazing animals.

The following signs usually indicate substantial improvement:-

> bright green, lush and even sward, dominated by grasses (though poaching causes unevenness);

> low diversity of forb species;

> more than 50% *Lolium perenne*, *Trifolium repens* and other agricultural species.

Fields which have been reseeded in the past and have since become somewhat more diverse are included in this category, but recently reseeded monoculture grassland such as rye grass leys, with or without clover, should be classified under cultivated land (J1). Most amenity grassland should also be classified under J1.

## B5  Marsh/marshy grassland

This is a diffuse category covering certain *Molinia* grasslands, grasslands with a high proportion of *Juncus* species, *Carex* species or *Filipendula ulmaria*, and wet meadows and pastures supporting communities of species such as *Caltha palustris* or *Valeriana* species, where broadleaved herbs rather than grasses, predominate. The category differs from swamp (F1) in that the latter has a water table distinctly above the substratum for much of the year and is dominated by reed grasses or large sedges. Unlike marginal vegetation (F2), marsh/marshy grassland occurs on more or less level areas, rather than on the banks of watercourses. It differs from flush (E2) in that bryophytes are not a conspicuous component of the vegetation, also flushes always have a flow or seepage of water through them.

The following communities are included in marsh/marshy grassland:-

> vegetation with a greater than 25% cover of *Molinia caerulea*, on less than 0.5m of peat (cf. mire, E);

> vegetation with less than 25% dwarf shrub cover on peat less than 0.5 m deep (cf. heathland, D);

> vegetation with a greater than 25% cover of *Juncus acutiflorus, J. effusus, J. inflexus, Carex* species or *Filipendula ulmaria*, except for grazed *Juncus effusus - Holcus lanatus/Deschampsia cespitosa* grasslands, which should be classified under neutral grassland, B2;

> wet meadows and pastures where grasses are subordinate to forbs (cf. wet neutral grassland, B2). Such communities are often rich in plants such as *Caltha palustris*, *Filipendula ulmaria*, *Valeriana* species, *Crepis paludosa*, *Dactylorhiza* species, *Eupatorium cannabinum*, *Juncus* species and *Carex* species.

If *Sphagnum* is abundant, refer to the mire classification (E).

## B6 Poor semi-improved grassland

Where there is a large amount of semi-improved grassland it may be useful to split this category into 'good semi-improved' and 'poor semi-improved', to facilitate re-survey of the better semi-improved grasslands at a later date. This sub-division is optional.

Good semi-improved grassland will have a reasonable diversity of herbaceous species, at least in parts of the sward, and is clearly recognisable as acid, calcareous or neutral in origin. Such grassland should be left in the semi-improved categories of acid, neutral and calcareous grassland (B1.2, 2.2 and 3.2). Poor semi-improved grassland will have a much more restricted list of species and, being more improved, it is more likely to resemble a species-poor neutral grassland, irrespective of its origin. This category (B6) should be marked SI and left uncoloured.

## C Tall herb and fern

### C1 Bracken

Areas dominated by *Pteridium aquilinum*, or with scattered patches of this species.

### C2 Upland species-rich ledges

This ledge vegetation contains species such as *Angelica sylvestris, Filipendula ulmaria, Solidago virgaurea, Athyrium filix-femina, Trollius europaeus* and *Crepis paludosa*. Areas supporting this habitat are nearly always too small to map and consequently must be target noted.

### C3 Other tall herb and fern

Tall ruderal (C3.1)

This category comprises stands of tall perennial or biennial dicotyledons, usually more than 25cm high, of species such as *Chamerion (Chamaenerion) angustifolium, Urtica dioica* and *Reynoutria japonica*. Dominant species should be coded. See also ephemeral/short perennial (J1).

Non-ruderal (C3.2)

Non-wooded stands of species such as *Oreopteris limbosperma, Athyrium felix-femina, Dryopteris* species or *Luzula sylvatica* should be included in this category. Dominant species should always be coded.

## D Heathland

Heathland includes vegetation dominated by ericoids or dwarf gorse species, as well as 'heaths' dominated by lichens and bryophytes, dwarf forbs, *Carex bigelowii* or *Juncus trifidus*. Generally occurring on well-drained acid soils, heathland is further distinguished from mire (E) by being arbitrarily defined as occurring on peat less than 0.5m thick (but see flood-plain mire E3.3). Dominant species should always be coded. See also dune heath (H6.6) and coastal heathland (H8.5).

### D1 Dry dwarf shrub heath

Vegetation with greater than 25% cover of ericoids or small gorse species in relatively dry situations forms this category. *Calluna vulgaris, Vaccinium myrtillus, Erica cinerea, Ulex minor* and *Ulex gallii* are typical of lowland dry dwarf shrub heath, whilst *Empetrum nigrum, Empetrum hermaphroditum, Arctostaphylos uva-ursi* and *Vaccinium vitis-idaea* are found in upland heaths. Acid heaths usually occur on deep podsols developed on base-deficient sands, gravels and clays. Basic heaths are much more restricted in extent, and may be recognised by the presence of herbs characteristic of chalk grassland and open habitats. See also wet dwarf shrub heath (D2), dry heath/acid grassland mosaic (D5) and dry modified bog (E1.4). Damp *Calluna* heath with

*Sphagnum capillifolium* (mainly in western Scotland) should be included in this category and target noted.

### D2    Wet dwarf shrub heath

As with dry dwarf shrub heath (D1), this vegetation type has more than 25% cover of ericoids and/or small *Ulex* species. However, it differs from D1 in that *Molinia caerulea* is often abundant and it generally contains some *Sphagnum compactum* or *Sphagnum tenellum* and less frequently other *Sphagna*. In transitions to mires, the proportion of *Sphagna* will increase and the species composition will change, often with *Sphagnum papillosum* and *Sphagnum subnitens* becoming more frequent. *Erica tetralix* is common in wet dwarf shrub heath and is often present in significant quantity. *Trichophorum cespitosum* is occasionally present at lower levels. Macrolichens such as *Cladonia portentosa* (*impexa*), *C. arbuscula* and *C. uncialis* may be locally abundant. The abundance of *Molinia* and *Erica tetralix* decreases in the transition from wet to dry heath. See also wet heath/acid grassland mosaic (D6) and wet modified bog (E1.3).

### D3    Lichen/bryophyte heath

This category comprises bryophyte and lichen-dominated heaths of mountain summits and lowland situations such as the East Anglian Breckland. Bryophytes and/or lichens must be dominant and there must be less than 30% vascular plant cover.

### D4    Montane heath/dwarf herb

This is a rather diverse grouping of montane heath and snow-bed vegetation types. Included in this category are heaths dominated by *Carex bigelowii* and *Juncus trifidus*, also dwarf forb communities of *Alchemilla alpina*, *Silene acaulis*, *Sibbaldia procumbens* and *Saxifraga* species. Montane dwarf shrub heath should not be included, but should be classified under D1 or D2; *Dryas octopetala* communities should be classified under calcareous grassland (B3).

### D5    Dry heath/acid grassland mosaic

This represents a common mixture of dry heath (D1) and acid grassland (B1), to be found on hill and moorland, and the category has been specified only for ease of mapping. The relative proportions of each type of habitat should be target noted.

### D6    Wet heath/acidic grassland mosaic

Vegetation mosaics similar to D5, but involving a mixture of wet heath (D2) with acid grassland (B1), make up this category. Again, the proportions of each habitat type should be target noted.

### E    Mire

Mires occur typically on deep peat (over 0.5 m thick) with the water table at or just below the surface, but flushes and springs on shallow or incipient peats are also included in this category.

The classification of peatlands has recently been revised (see NCC 1989) and the term bog is now restricted to ombrotrophic mires (blanket bog and raised bog), which are fed only by direct precipitation, unlike minerotrophic mires - fens (valley, flood-plain and basin mires), flushes and springs - which are fed by ground water or streams. The distinction between ombrotrophic and minerotrophic mires is not always clear-cut and transitional examples should be target-noted. Furthermore, areas of minerotrophic mire may occur within blanket and raised mires; likewise, ombrotrophic areas may occur locally within fens. Examples of these should be target noted, but may be included within the major mire type for mapping purposes.

### E1    Bog

Unmodified bog (blanket bog and raised bog) consists of *Sphagnum*-rich vegetation, lying on peat more than 0.5 m deep, with the water table at or just below the surface and no input of water from the surrounding land. Modified bog contains little or no *Sphagnum*.

#### Blanket bog (E1.6.1)

Blanket bog comprises *Sphagnum*-rich vegetation on deep peat, forming a blanket over both concave and convex surfaces, on level to moderately sloping ground in the uplands. It is widespread in the north and west of Britain, where it may be fragmentary or very extensive. The drainage is usually diffuse and undisturbed blanket bog often shows a hummock-and-hollow structure, with *Sphagnum*-rich pools in the hollows. Blanket bog includes watershed mires, saddle mires, terrace bog and valleyside mire and may also include other mire types, where these occur within a blanket bog complex.

This habitat category is used for relatively undamaged blanket bog, with *Sphagnum* usually abundant (typically *Sphagnum papillosum*, together with other species such as *Sphagnum magellanicum*). A wide range of ericoids, including *Calluna vulgaris*, *Erica tetralix*, *Vaccinium* species and *Empetrum* species, may be present, mainly on the hummocks, together with *Eriophorum vaginatum*, *Eriophorum angustifolium* and *Trichophorum cespitosum*. *Calluna* and/or *Eriophorum vaginatum* are often dominant over large areas, but various mixtures of species occur. Dominant species should be coded. Bog pool systems and areas of peat cutting, often characterised by the presence of *Sphagnum recurvum*, should be target noted or mapped as open water (G1.4) or bare peat (E4) if sufficiently large.

Significantly damaged blanket bog, in which

*Sphagnum* is much reduced or absent, should be classified as modified bog (E1.7 or E1.8).

### Raised bog (E1.6.2)

Raised bogs are found on estuarine flats, river flood plains and other level areas with impeded drainage in the lowlands, also at moderate altitudes, where they may grade into blanket mire. Many raised bogs overlie sites of glacial lakes which became infilled. In a classic raised bog, a structure now rare in Britain, the peat is several metres deep and has accumulated to form a distinctly raised dome, with peat depth greatest in the centre and decreasing towards the edges, which are marked by the more steeply sloping mire margin. Drainage tends to flow around the mire, forming a lagg stream, and the drier sloping margins of the mire may carry lagg woodland, which should be mapped as woodland.

Undamaged raised bog vegetation is very similar to that described under blanket bog (E1.6.1). Modification of raised bogs by draining, burning and peat-cutting can lead to the formation of wet modified bog and dry modified bog, which should be mapped as E1.7 or E1.8.

### Wet modified bog (E1.7)

This category comprises modified bog vegetation with little or no *Sphagnum*, often with bare peat and patches of *Trichophorum cespitosum* and/or *Molinia caerulea*. Ericoids may be abundant, sparse or absent.

This vegetation is mainly found on drying and degraded blanket bogs and cut-over raised bogs. It may resemble wet heath (D2), but is distinguished by having a peat depth greater than 0.5 m. *Molinia*-dominated vegetation on deep peat is included in this category rather than in marshy grassland (B5).

### Dry modified bog (E1.8)

The vegetation of dry modified bog is dominated by *Calluna vulgaris* and other ericoids, or by *Eriophorum vaginatum*, on peat more than 0.5m deep. *Sphagnum* is notably absent, but under the dwarf shrubs there may be a carpet of hypnoid mosses, with lichens such as *Cladonia portentosa* and *Cladonia arbuscula*. Where *Eriophorum vaginatum* is dominant, as on many Pennine blanket bogs, other species may be sparse or absent. Essentially dry heath vegetation (or cotton-grass moor) on deep peat, this habitat type is typical of areas of blanket bog or raised bog subjected to heavy grazing, burning and draining.

## E2   Flush and spring

These types of minerotrophic mire are termed soligenous because they are associated with water movement. They may or may not form peat, but where they do, the peat is often less than 0.5 m deep. Flushes occur on gently-sloping ground, are often linear or triangular and may include small watercourses. They may be extensive or too small to map, in which case they should be target noted. Where flushes feed a fen (E3) they should be target noted and mapped as an integral part of the mire complex, unless they are very large and distinct, when they may be individually mapped.

Flushes typically have an open or closed ground layer of *Sphagnum* and/or other bryophytes, together with small sedges and *Juncus* species. The presence of a well developed bryophyte ground layer and the lack of dominant grasses distinguishes flush habitats from marshy grassland and from wet acid, neutral and calcareous grasslands. Thus, a habitat with *Juncus effusus* over herbs and grasses is a marsh/marshy grassland (B5). Complex mosaics of grassland and flush are quite common, particularly in the uplands, and should be mapped according to the most prevalent habitat, with the proportions of each recorded in a target note.

Flushes may be acid, neutral (mesotrophic) or basic. These categories are not always easy to distinguish. In cases of doubt use the magenta colour code only and target note.

### Acid/neutral flush (E2.1)

These typically support species-poor vegetation consisting of a *Sphagnum* carpet overlain by *Carex* or *Juncus* species. Characteristic moss species include *Sphagnum recurvum*, *S. palustre* and *S. auriculatum*. Overlying vegetation may consist of small *Carex* species (*Carex echinata*, *C. nigra* or *C. curta*), *Carex rostrata*, *Juncus acutiflorus*, *J. effusus*, *J. squarrosus*, or *Eriophorum angustifolium*. Dominant species should be coded.

### Basic flush (E2.2)

Basic flushes typically support a carpet of pleurocarpous brown mosses, often without *Sphagnum*, overlain by a conspicuous small sedge layer, *Carex flacca*, *Schoenus nigricans* or a mixed-herb layer. Characteristic pleurocarpous mosses include *Scorpidium*, *Campylium*, *Drepanocladus* and *Calliergon* species, whilst characteristic herbs include *Eleocharis quinqueflora*, *Eriophorum latifolium* and *Carex lepidocarpa*.

### Bryophyte-dominated spring (E2.3)

This habitat occurs only in the immediate vicinity of up-wellings and it usually consists of spongy mats or small mounds dominated by bryophytes such as *Cratoneuron* or *Philonotis* species. Areas which fall within this category are normally too small to map and should be target noted. Flushes occurring downslope of a spring should be mapped if they are large enough.

## E3   Fen

Fens are defined as minerotrophic mires, usually over peat more than 0.5 m deep (but see E3.3). The water table is at or just below the surface.

Three main types of fen can be distinguished, using topographical rather than vegetational criteria. These are valley mire, which, because there is obvious water flow, is classified as soligenous, and basin and flood-plain mires, which have impeded drainage and are termed topogenous. However, the distinction between these three mire types is not always clear in the field, so for Phase 1 mapping purposes their identification is optional.

'Poor fen' contains acid water (pH 5 or less) and short vegetation with a high proportion of *Sphagnum*. 'Rich fen' contains more calcareous water (pH above 5), *Sphagnum* is often absent and the vegetation usually includes patches of tall plants and species such as *Juncus subnodulosus*, *Schoenus nigricans* and *Carex lepidocarpa*, characteristic of base-rich situations. Where acid or basic fen can be identified, this should be made clear in a target note and basic fen should be indicated by the code 'B'.

Where there are very wet areas containing tall swamp vegetation such as *Phragmites australis* or large sedges, these should be target noted as swamp (F1), or marked as patches of sky blue, if large enough to map within the area delineated as fen. Parts of the mire dominated by marsh (fen meadow) or carr should be mapped or target noted as grassland (B5), woodland (A1) or scrub (A2). Springs and small flushes which feed or lie within a fen, should be treated as an integral part of the mire system and target noted (see E2). Areas of bog within a fen and patches of degraded fen should also be target noted.

### Valley mire (E3.1)

A valley mire develops along the lower slopes and floor of a small valley and receives water from springs and seepages on the valley sides, feeding a central watercourse. Such a fen can be distinguished from a flush because the former is a complex, whereas a flush is a discrete single feature, usually of limited extent.

Valley mires are often dominated by acidophilous vegetation containing *Sphagnum* species, *Carex* species and ericoids. However, vegetation typical of base-rich conditions can also occur, for instance *Schoenus nigricans* and *Juncus subnodulosus*. Floating mats of mosses and sedges may be present. Acid watercourses often contain *Hypericum elodes* and *Potamogeton polygonifolius*.

### Basin mire (E3.2)

This type of fen develops in a waterlogged basin and contains very little open water. The water table within the basin is level, but small flushes may occur around the edges and there is a limited through-flow of water.

The vegetation may be dominated by *Sphagnum* species, together with *Carex rostrata* and ericoids, or by tall swamp plants such as *Phragmites australis*, *Schoenoplectus* (*Scirpus*) *lacustris*, *Typha* species and, in base-rich situations, *Cladium mariscus*.

### Flood-plain mire (E3.3)

This type of fen forms on a river or stream flood-plain which is waterlogged and, typically, inundated periodically. The substrate may be peat, mineral or a mixture of both. The range of vegetation types is similar to that of a basin mire (E3.2).

## E4    Bare peat

Patches of bare peat more than 0.25 ha in extent (that is, approximately 50 m x 50 m) should be mapped. Peat hagging and areas of eroding peat haggs should be target noted. Commercial peat-workings are included in this category.

## F    Swamp, marginal and inundation

This habitat category is defined as emergent or frequently inundated vegetation, occurring over peat or mineral soils. The depth of water at the time of survey, or seasonal variation in water level, if known, should be target noted, also the nature of the substrate. Note that this category differs from mire (E) and from marsh/marshy grassland (B5) in having the water table distinctly above the level of the substrate for most of the year.

## F1    Swamp

Swamp contains tall emergent vegetation typical of the transition between open water and exposed land. Swamps are generally in standing water for a large part of the year, but may occasionally be found on substrates that are seldom immersed, as in the later stages of the seral succession to marshy grassland.

Species composition varies according to the trophic status of the water, the substrate type, etc. Note that vegetation dominated by *Molinia caerulea*, *Filipendula ulmaria*, mosses, small *Carex* species or *Juncus* species, should be classified as marsh/marshy grassland (B5) or flush (E2), as appropriate. Swamp vegetation includes both mixed and single-species stands of *Typha* species, *Phragmites australis*; *Phalaris arundinacea*, *Glyceria maxima*, *Carex paniculata*, *C. acutiformis*, *C. rostrata* or other tall sedge. Single-species stands are usually found in deeper water and should be indicated with species codes.

Strips of swamp vegetation narrower than 5m bordering watercourses should be classified as marginal vegetation (F2.1).

## F2    Marginal and Inundation

### Marginal vegetation (F2.1)

This category encompasses all narrow strips of emergent vegetation occurring on the (often steep) margins of lowland watercourses, where the water table is permanently high. Bands of tall vegetation wider than 5 m should be classified as swamp (F1). Marginal vegetation is typically open and contains plants such as *Glyceria* species, *Rorippa* species, *Apium nodiflorum*, *Berula erecta*, *Oenanthe* species, *Galium palustre*, *Nasturtium officinale*, *Myosotis* species, *Veronica* species, *Alisma* species, *Sparganium erectum*, *Carex riparia*, *Juncus effusus* and *Juncus inflexus*, also small stands of taller plants such as *Phragmites australis*, *Typha* species and *Phalaris arundinacea*. Areas of such vegetation will be too small to map, so should be target noted.

### Inundation vegetation (F2.2)

This category includes open and innately unstable communities that are subject to periodic inundation, as found on sorted or unsorted silts, sands and gravels of river beds and islands and on the draw-down zone around pools, lakes and reservoirs. A wide variety of species occur in such communities, including *Polygonum* species, *Juncus bulbosus*, *Bidens* species, *Agrostis stolonifera* and *Alopecurus geniculatus*, as well as many ruderal species.

## G    Open water

Open water is defined as water lying beyond the limits of swamp or emergent vegetation, although it may contain submerged, free-floating or floating-leaved vegetation. The dominant species of any such vegetation should be coded, and the salinity of the water, whether fresh or brackish, indicated if possible. Where aquatic vegetation is present in quantity but there is insufficient room to code all abundant species, a target note should be provided. For those wishing to provide details of the trophic status of the water, Table 10 gives the characteristics of each type (see also Palmer 1989).

### G1    Standing water

Standing water includes lakes, reservoirs, pools, flooded gravel pits, ponds, water-filled ditches, canals and brackish lagoons.

### G2    Running water

Running water comprises rivers and streams. The direction of flow should be indicated by an arrow. If survey is needed at a more detailed level than for Phase 1, refer to *Surveys of wildlife in river corridors* (NCC 1985). This draft methodology includes a comprehensive classification of bank and open water habitats, a recording card and instructions on the preparation of habitat maps.

## H    Coastland

Coastal lagoons should be classified as standing water (G1.6).

### H1    Intertidal

The codes for *Zostera*, green algal beds or brown algal beds should, where appropriate, be superimposed over the relevant Ordnance Survey symbols (mud/sand; shingle/cobbles; boulders/rocks).

### H2    Saltmarsh

#### Saltmarsh/dune interface (H2.3)

Vegetation peculiar to this area, characterised by species such as *Frankenia laevis* or *Suaeda fruticosa*, should be mapped wherever large enough, and always target noted.

#### Scattered plants (H2.4)

The dominant species should be coded.

#### Dense/continuous (H2.6)

Dominant species should be coded, particularly noting *Spartina* where it is abundant. Areas of inland saltmarsh should be included in this category.

### H3    Shingle/gravel above high-tide mark

Target note any vascular plants or lichen vegetation that may occur.

### H4    Boulders/rocks above high-tide mark

Target note as for H3.

### H5    Strandline vegetation

This type of vegetation occurs as an open community on the drift line and is characterised by species such as *Cakile maritima*, *Honkenya peploides*, *Rumex crispus*, *Salsola kali*, *Atriplex* species and *Beta vulgaris* ssp. *maritima*. In contrast to fore dunes, *Elymus farctus* (*Agropyron junceiforme*) is characteristically sparse or absent. Target note where feasible, stating whether the substrate is shingle or rock.

### H6    Sand dune

#### Dune slack (H6.4)

Dune slacks are valleys or hollows between dune ridges, where the water table is close to the surface for at least several months in the year, leading to marshy vegetation. *Ammophila arenaria* is usually absent. Characteristic species are *Salix repens*, *Hydrocotyle vulgaris*, *Dactylorhiza* species and *Epipactis palustris*. Saline slacks should be classified as saltmarsh (H2).

#### Dune grassland (H6.5)

All grassland occurring on consolidated and flattened dunes should be classified in this category. Generally, little *Ammophila arenaria* will be present. Machair should be included here.

# Table 10 Classification of standing and running waters

| | Physical characteristics | Typical plant species |
|---|---|---|
| 1 Eutrophic | Water often strongly discoloured by algae. pH usually over 7. Substrate often highly organic mud. | *Lemna* spp.<br>*Myriophyllum spicatum*<br>*Potamogeton pectinatus*<br>*Ceratophyllum* spp.<br>*Zannichellia palustris*<br>*Ranunculus circinatus*<br>*Polygonum amphibium*<br>*Chara* spp.<br>*Nuphar lutea*<br>*Ranunculus penicillatus* var. *calcareus* is typical of flowing waters |
| 2 Mesotrophic | Water sometimes discoloured by planktonic algae. pH usually around or slightly below neutral | *Potamogeton gramineus*<br>*P. obtusifolius*<br>*P. perfoliatus*<br>*Callitriche hermaphroditica*<br>*Nitella* spp.<br>*Nuphar lutea*<br>*Nymphaea alba* |
| 3 Oligotrophic | Water very clear, plankton sparse. pH usually less than 7. Substrate rocky, sandy or peaty. | *Potamogeton polygonifolius*<br>*Myriophyllum alterniflorum*<br>*Juncus bulbosus*<br>*Scirpus fluitans*<br>*Subularia aquatica*<br>*Lobelia dortmanna*<br>*Isoetes lacustris*<br>*Sparganium angustifolium*<br>*Callitriche hamulata*.<br>Flowing waters dominated by bryophytes. |
| 4 Dystrophic | Water usually peat-stained. pH very low (3.5 - 5.5). Alkalinity very low (up to 2mg/l $CaCO_3$) | *Sphagnum* spp.<br>*Juncus bulbosus*<br>*Potamogeton polygonifolius*<br>Macrophyte flora very restricted. |
| 5 Marl/tufa | May be eutrophic, mesotrophic or (very rarely) oligotrophic. Water very clear. Alkalinity at least 100mg/l $CaCo_3$. Powdery yellow-brown deposit of marl covers substrate in lakes. Highly calcareous streams deposit tufa. | *Chara* spp.<br>*Myriophyllum spicatum*<br>*Potamogeton lucens* |
| 6 Brackish | Most brackish systems are coastal, but a few are inland, with salinity derived from artificial sources such as mine drainage, or from residues of ancient marine incursions in peaty areas. Conductivity 1,250 to 50,000 μmhos. | Flora very restricted.<br>Slightly saline waters -<br>  *Potamogeton pectinatus*<br>  *P. pusillus*<br>  *Myriophyllum spicatum*<br>  *Zannichellia palustris*<br>  *Ceratophyllum submersum*<br>  *Ranunculus baudotii*<br>  *Enteromorpha* spp.<br>More saline waters -<br>  *Ruppia* spp, fucoids, *Zostera* spp. |

### Dune heath (H6.6)

All heathland occurring on consolidated and flattened dunes should be included in this category. *Calluna* is usually the dominant ericoid, with *Erica cinerea* and *Erica tetralix* also common. *Carex arenaria* is often present and lichens, particularly *Cladonia* species, are often abundant. Occasionally, juniper may be present. Use yellow crosses for scattered heath.

### Dune scrub (H6.7)

All scrub occurring on consolidated and flattened dunes should be classified in this category. *Hippophae rhamnoides* is a characteristic species. Use green crosses for scattered scrub.

### Open dune (H6.8)

This category comprises the three early successional stages of dune formation, less stable and with lower vegetation cover than H6.4-H6.7.

> Fore dune: unstable, usually low ridges of sand on the foreshore, often with a very open plant cover. *Elymus farctus* is strongly characteristic, often dominant, and sometimes the only species present; *Honkenya peploides*, *Atriplex* species and *Cakile maritima* are typical associated species; *Ammophila arenaria* may be present in small quantities, but should not be dominant.

> Yellow dune: partially stabilized ridges of sand lying between fore and grey dunes, with a marked but incomplete plant cover, nearly always dominated by *Ammophila arenaria*, although *Leymus* (*Elymus*) *arenarius* and/or *Elymus farctus* may be common; a variety of small herbs may be present.

> Grey dune: stable ridges of sand, almost completely vegetated. The vegetation is very variable in species composition; *Ammophila arenaria* is usually present, but not dominant, mosses and lichens may be frequent. Grey dune can be distinguished from fixed dune by being markedly hilly or undulating, and by the sand not being fully consolidated.

## H8    Maritime cliff and slope

### Maritime hard cliff (H8.1)

These are cliffs formed of rock (including chalk) with less than 10% vascular plant cover. The type of rock should be target noted. Vegetated cliffs should be mapped using the relevant vegetation code and target noted.

### Maritime soft cliff (H8.2)

These are cliffs formed of mud or clay with less than 10% vascular plant cover. The type of substrate should be target noted.

### Crevice and ledge vegetation (H8.3)

This category comprises vegetation, occasionally sparse, but covering at least 10% of the cliff surface, occurring in crevices or on ledges on steep cliffs. The communities present should be described with a target note, taking care to record whether the vegetation is influenced by the use of the cliffs by birds, as may be indicated by species such as *Beta vulgaris*. Vegetation occurring in the splash zone at the base of cliffs should be included here.

### Coastal grassland (H8.4)

These are grasslands which include maritime species and which occur on shallow slopes or level areas by the sea, often on cliff tops (but see dune grassland - H6.5). Indicator species include *Scilla verna*, *Plantago maritima* and *Armeria maritima*. *Festuca rubra* is often dominant. Other species may include *Hieracium pilosella*, *Anthyllis vulneraria*, *Lotus corniculatus*, *Galium verum* and *Thymus praecox*.

### Coastal heathland (H8.5)

All heathlands which include maritime species and which occur on shallow slopes, or even level areas, by the sea should be included in this category (but see dune heath - H6.6). Indicator species include *Scilla verna*, *Armeria maritima*, *Jasione montana*, *Plantago maritima* and *Plantago coronopus*. *Calluna vulgaris* is often dominant; *Erica cinerea* and dwarf *Ulex* species are frequently present. Coastal heathland often occurs just inland of coastal grassland, and like that category, frequently occurs at the top of cliffs.

## I    Rock exposure and waste

This grouping includes both natural and artificial exposed rock surfaces where these are almost entirely lacking in vegetation, as well as various forms of excavations and waste tips. Significant communities of mosses, lichens and ferns growing on walls or rock ledges should be target noted. See also maritime cliff and slope (H8).

## I1    Natural exposures

### Inland cliff (I1.1)

This category is defined as rock surfaces over 2 m high and sloping at more than 60°. Vegetated cliffs with more than 10% vascular plant cover are not included, but should be mapped using the relevant vegetation code, and target noted as necessary.

### Scree (I1.2)

Scree is defined as an accumulation, usually at the foot of a cliff, of weathered rock fragments of all sizes, mostly angular in shape. This category includes large boulders (boulder scree) which should be mapped using enlarged red dots.

### Limestone pavement (I1.3)

This comprises a near horizontal surface, usually of Carboniferous Limestone, which is irregularly corrugated and furrowed by solution and often cut by deeper and more regular fissures (grikes), which correspond to naturally occurring joints within the rock.

### Other exposure (I1.4)

Exposed rock on mountain tops and in river beds should, for example, be included in this category.

### Cave (I1.5)

Any natural recess, large enough to enter and with a complete ceiling, should be mapped as cave and any features of interest target noted. Large crevices and deep narrow gullies should not be included here, but should be mapped under 'other'.

## I2 Artificial exposures and waste tips

The boundaries of quarries, spoil heaps, mines or refuse tips should be outlined in red. Covering vegetation, if abundant, should be coded as appropriate, under grassland, scrub, etc, or target noted if sparse.

### Quarry (I2.1)

Excavations such as gravel, sand or chalk pits and stone quarries should be included in this category. Target note the mineral or ore which has been, or is being, extracted. If the site is water-filled, map as open water and target note previous use.

### Spoil (I2.2)

Includes abandoned industrial areas and tips of waste material such as coal mine spoil and slag. Spoil heaps within quarries should be included in I2.1. Target note the type of spoil.

### Mine (I2.3)

Mark the area on the map and target note any features of interest.

### Refuse-tip (I2.4)

Target note any vegetation of interest, if it covers an area too small to map, and code the dominant species.

## J Miscellaneous

Features such as parks, gardens, golf courses and railway cuttings or embankments are not listed as separate habitat types, since they are clearly marked as such on Ordnance Survey maps. The colour codes for the appropriate habitat type (for example grassland, woodland or scrub) should, however, be superimposed over the feature on the Ordnance Survey map.

## J1 Cultivated/disturbed land

### Arable (J1.1)

This includes arable cropland, horticultural land (for example nurseries, vegetable plots, flower beds), freshly-ploughed land and recently reseeded grassland, such as rye grass and rye-clover leys, often managed for silage.

### Amenity grassland (J1.2)

This comprises intensively managed and regularly mown grasslands, typical of lawns, playing fields, golf course fairways and many urban 'savannah' parks, in which *Lolium perenne*, with or without *Trifolium repens*, often predominates. The sward composition will depend on the original seed mixture used and on the age of the community. Herbs such as *Bellis perennis*, *Plantago major* and *Taraxacum officinale* may be present. If the amenity grassland has a sward rich in herbs, it may be possible to classify it as semi-improved acidic, neutral or calcareous grassland, as appropriate. In such cases, the area concerned should be mapped as the specific grassland type and its amenity use target noted.

### Ephemeral/short perennial (J1.3)

Short, patchy plant associations typical of derelict urban sites, quarries and railway ballast, should be classified here. The land must be freely draining, and usually has shallow stony soil. The vegetation typically lacks a clear dominant species, but consists of a mixture of low-growing plants, often less than 25 cm high, such as *Plantago major*, *Ranunculus repens*, *Trifolium repens*, *Medicago lupulina*, *Tussilago farfara*, *Leucanthemum vulgare* and *Senecio* species, or of taller species such as *Sisymbrium* or *Melilotus* species. Parts of fields containing similar communities, such as areas around gates, should not be included, but should be classified as grassland (B). See also tall ruderal (C3.1).

### Introduced shrub (J1.4)

This is vegetation dominated by shrub species that are not locally native, whether planted or self-sown. Common introduced shrubs include species of *Buxus*, *Cornus*, *Laurus*, *Ligustrum*, *Rhododendron* and *Symphoricarpus*. Formal beds of shrubs such as of *Hypericum calycinum*, *Cotoneaster*, heaths and dwarf conifers should be included here. Introduced shrubs forming an understorey in woodland should be mapped as woodland (A1) and target noted. Introduced shrub on sand dunes should be classified as dune scrub (H6.7). See also scrub (A2).

## J2 Boundaries

Although a key to field boundaries is supplied, time constraints often preclude the mapping of boundaries. Nevertheless, the conservation value of hedges should not be overlooked and it is recommended that at least the better examples should be mapped and target noted, particularly in lowland areas. Species-rich hedges should be differentiated from species-poor ones by the use of the zig-zag symbol. Fences are usually of little significance, as their wildlife value is low, but recording new boundaries and removed boundaries may be important. A clear decision should be made as to the types of boundary to be mapped and consistency should be maintained.

Guidance on recording grassy road verges, railway cuttings and embankments is given under the grassland section (B). Where they are dominated by trees or scrub they should be categorised as woodland (A) and mapped if very broad, otherwise simply target noted.

### Intact hedge (J2.1)

Intact hedges are entire and more-or-less stock-proof.

### Defunct hedge (J2.2)

Hedges in which there are gaps and which are no longer stock-proof fall into this category.

### Hedgerow with trees (J2.3)

The frequency of cross-hatching should be varied to indicate the density of trees. Windbreaks should be classified under A3.

### Species-rich hedges (J2.4)

These have a diversity of native woody species and a good hedgerow bottom flora.

### Wall (J2.5)

Significant communities of mosses, lichens or ferns growing on walls may be target noted, particularly in built-up areas.

### Ditch (J2.6)

Only ditches which appear to be dry for most of the year should be included in this category. Wet ditches are mapped as standing water (G1) or possibly swamp (F1).

### Boundary removed (J2.7)

Use spaced crosses on the appropriate Ordnance Survey symbol.

### Earth bank (J2.8)

The ditch/bank systems found on ancient woodland sites may be included here, as should sea walls constructed of natural materials.

## J3 Built-up areas

### Caravan site (J3.4)

Hatching may be used as an overlay on the appropriate semi-natural habitat colour, for instance where the site is on coastal grassland or in woodland.

### Sea wall (J3.5)

Only sea walls constructed of artificial materials (for example concrete) should be included here. Others should be mapped as earth banks (J2.8).

### Buildings (J3.6)

Map unmarked new buildings or built-up areas and colour those already shown on the Ordnance Survey maps. Agricultural, industrial and domestic buildings should all be coloured in solid black. There is no need to distinguish between them.

## J4 Bare ground

Any type of bare soil or other substrate should be included here where not already covered (compare bare peat E4, intertidal H1, shingle H3, boulders and rocks H4, Dunes H6, maritime cliff H8 and natural rock exposure I). Target note extensive or otherwise important areas of bare ground.

## J5 Other habitat

Draw a black line around any habitat not encompassed by the classification and describe it in a target note.

# Acknowledgements

This manual is a revision of NCC's draft Habitat mapping manual (Phase 1), produced in 1986 by Robert Wolton. This was based on the original methodology devised by Ian Bonner in 1974 and developed by Tim Bines and Peter Welsh, of the England Field Unit, in 1982 and 1983. After wide consultation within the NCC, an initial revision of the 1986 draft was produced in 1989 by Carol Blake.

Since then, the manual has been thoroughly revised by Peter Kelly and Margaret Palmer, to bring it into line with current survey practice in the NCC and to improve the habitat classification and definitions.

Many people have been consulted over the period of years in which this manual has been in preparation and all have freely given their time and advice. Thanks are due to Dr H Ash (St Helens and Knowsley survey), Dr R G H Bunce (Institute of Terrestrial Ecology), I Collis (West Midlands County Council), Dr M Game (Greater London Council), J Green (Grampian Regional Council survey), Dr J F Handley (Groundwork Trust), R Hobs (Norfolk Naturalists Trust), D Nicholls (Leicester City Wildlife Project), J A Spalton (Norfolk Survey), C Steel (Devon Trust for Nature Conservation), D Stubbs (London Wildlife Trust survey) and Dr B J Trowbridge (Woodland Trust), all of whom advised on the preparation of the draft version.

Further helpful comment and advice have been received from the many users of the draft version, in particular from Tim Blackstock, Ann Greatrex, Lindsay Kinnes, Liz Pulford, Denise Ramsay, and Greg Smith.

# References

ASH, H. J. & GATELEY, P. 1984. Urban botanical survey: draft report. St Helens, Merseyside, The Groundwork Grust.

BAKER, J.R. & DRUMMOND, J.E. 1984. Environmental monitoring and map revision using integrated LANDSAT and digital cartographic data. ITC Journal, 1, 10-19.

BALL, S.G. 1988. RECORDER, a biological recording package for Local Record Centres. (Advanced Revelation Version). Peterborough, Nature Conservancy Council.

CANFIELD, R.H. 1941. Application of the line-intercept method in sampling range vegetation. J. Forestry, 39, 388-394.

CLAPHAM, A.R., TUTIN, T.G. & MOORE, D.M. 1987. Flora of the British Isles, 3rd ed. Cambridge, Cambridge University Press.

CLAPHAM, A.R., TUTIN, T.G. & WARBURG, E.F. 1981. Excursion flora of the British Isles, 3rd ed. Cambridge, Cambridge University Press.

DONY, J.G., JURY, S.L. & PERRING, F. 1986. English names of wild flowers, 2nd ed. Reading, Botanical Society of the British Isles.

EVANS, C. 1988. Habitat classification manual. Reserves Ecology Department, Royal Society for the Protection of Birds.

GAME, M. 1984. A strategic survey of London's wildlife habitats. Unpublished note on methodology and on survey uses and limitations. London, Transportation and Development Department, Greater London Council.

KELLY, P.G., & PERRY, K.P. In prep. Wildlife habitat in Cumbria. (Research and Survey in Nature Conservation series). Peterborough, Nature Conservancy Council.

KIRBY, K.J., PETERKEN, G.F., SPENCER, J.W. & WALKER, G.J. 1984. Inventories of ancient semi-natural woodland. (Focus on Nature Conservation, No. 6). Peterborough, Nature Conservancy Council.

NCC. 1977. Methods of locating old herb-rich grasslands. (GB studies on SSSI criteria, Nc. 1). Unpublished report by J E Forbes, Nature Conservancy Council.

NCC. 1979a. Description of Phase 1 broad ecological survey and land use mapping, as used in south east Scotland, Cumbria and parts of West Yorkshire. Unpublished paper by I. Bonner. Nature Conservancy Council.

NCC. 1979b. Land use/habitat survey (Phase 1), revised version. Unpublished paper. NW England Region, Nature Conservancy Council.

NCC. 1980. Lowland agricultural habitats (Scotland): Air-photo analysis of change. (CST Report No 332). I Langdale-Brown, S Jennings, C L Crawford, G M Jolly and J Muscott. Unpublished. Nature Conservancy Council.

NCC. 1982. The standard habitat classification for use in NCC for the mapping and description of SSSIs. Unpublished paper. England Field Unit, Nature Conservancy Council.

NCC. 1983a. Selection of biological SSSI. Policy & Procedure Guidelines. NCC/P83/19G. Unpublished, Nature Conservancy Council.

NCC. 1983b. Phase 1 survey, habitat classification and mapping codes. Unpublished paper. NW England Region, Nature Conservancy Council.

NCC. 1983c. Phase 1 land use and habitat survey of Somerset (1983). D Howlett, J Williamson, H Tripp, A Burdett, D Burton, D Chown, M Elliot and C Pulteney. Unpublished. SW England Region, Nature Conservancy Council.

NCC. 1983d. Phase 1 land use and habitat survey of Dorset (1983). A Swash, I Alexander, P Christian, D Exton, P Harvey and T Warrick. Unpublished. SW England Region, Nature Conservancy Council.

NCC. 1984. Nature conservation in Great Britain. Peterborough, Nature Conservancy Council.

NCC. 1985. Surveys of wildlife in river corridors: draft methodology. Unpublished report. Nature Conservancy Council.

NCC. 1986a. Phase 1 survey of Cumbria: 1 Carlisle District. Unpublished report by P Kelly, R Jerram, J Hooson & A Kyle. NW Region, Nature Conservancy Council.

NCC. 1986b. Habitat mapping manual (Phase 1). Unpublished draft by Nature Conservancy Council.

NCC. 1987. Changes in the Cumbrian countryside. First report of the National Countryside Monitoring Scheme. (Research and survey in nature conservation, No. 6.) Peterborough, Nature Conservancy Council.

NCC. 1988. National Countryside Monitoring Scheme, Scotland: Grampian. Battleby, Perth, Countryside Commission for Scotland and Nature Conservancy Council.

NCC. 1989. Guidelines for selection of biological SSSIs. Peterborough, Nature Conservancy Council.

NCC/RSNC. 1984. NCC/RSNC habitat classification. Unpublished paper. Royal Society for Nature Conservation and Nature Conservancy Council.

PALMER, M.A. 1989. A botanical classification of standing waters in Great Britain. (Research and survey in Nature Conservation, No 19). Peterborough, Nature Conservancy Council.

RAMSAY, D.B. 1985. Cheshire habitat survey analysis. Unpublished report. Country Planning Department. Cheshire County Council.

RATCLIFFE, D.A., ed. 1977. A nature conservation review. Cambridge, Cambridge University Press.

RODWELL, J. in prep. British plant communities 5 vols. Cambridge, Cambridge University Press. (National Vegetation Classification.)

SHIMWELL, D. 1983. A conspectus of urban vegetation types. University of Manchester. Unpublished report to Nature Conservancy Council.

USHER, M.B., ed. 1986. Wildlife conservation evaluation. London, Chapman and Hall.

WIGAN MBC. 1987. Wigan Metropolitan Borough Phase 1 survey. Unpublished report. Wigan Metropolitan Borough Council.

Appendix one

# Phase 1 survey
# habitat classification,
# hierarchical alphanumeric
# reference codes
# and
# mapping colour codes

## A  Woodland and scrub

**1 Woodland**

   1 Broad-leaved

      1 Semi-natural  Green

      2 Plantation  Green

   2 Coniferous

      1 Semi-natural  True green

      2 Plantation  True green

   3 Mixed

      1 Semi-natural  Green over true green

      2 Plantation  Green and true green

**2 Scrub**

   1 Dense/continuous  Green

   2 Scattered  Green

**3 Parkland/scattered trees**

   *1 Broad-leaved  Green

   *2 Coniferous  True green

   *3 Mixed  Green and true green

**4 Recently-felled woodland**

   *1 Broad-leaved  Green

   *2 Coniferous  True green

   *3 Mixed  Green and true green

## B  Grassland and marsh

**1 Acid grassland**

   1 Unimproved  Orange

   2 Semi-improved  Orange

**2 Neutral grassland**

   1 Unimproved  Orange

   2 Semi-improved  Orange

**3 Calcareous grassland**

   1 Unimproved  Orange

   2 Semi-improved   Orange

**4 Improved grassland**  No colour

**5 Marsh/marshy grassland**  Purple over orange

**\*6 Poor semi-improved grassland** (optional)    SI    No colour

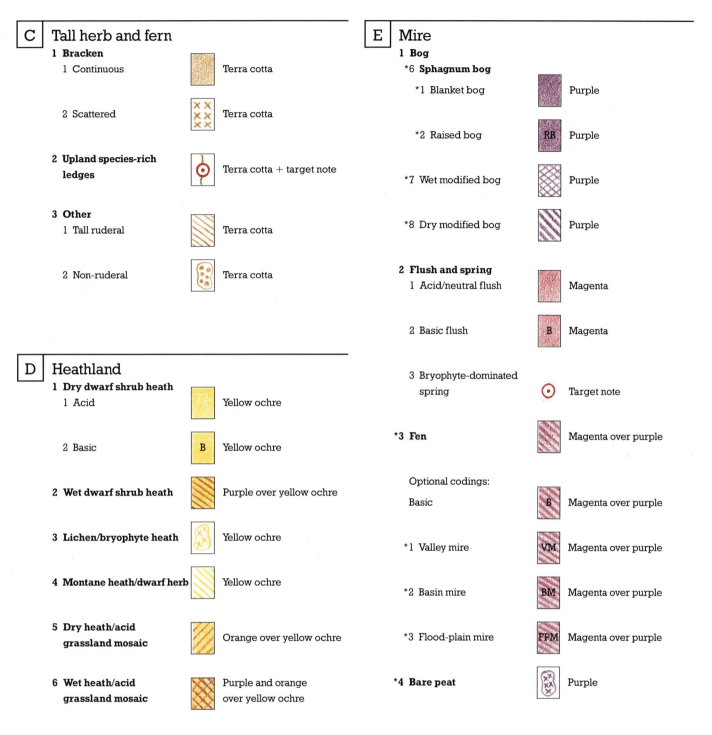

| | | |
|---|---|---|
| **C** Tall herb and fern | | |
| 1 **Bracken** | | |
|   1 Continuous | | Terra cotta |
|   2 Scattered | | Terra cotta |
| 2 **Upland species-rich ledges** | | Terra cotta + target note |
| 3 **Other** | | |
|   1 Tall ruderal | | Terra cotta |
|   2 Non-ruderal | | Terra cotta |
| **D** Heathland | | |
| 1 **Dry dwarf shrub heath** | | |
|   1 Acid | | Yellow ochre |
|   2 Basic | | Yellow ochre |
| 2 **Wet dwarf shrub heath** | | Purple over yellow ochre |
| 3 **Lichen/bryophyte heath** | | Yellow ochre |
| 4 **Montane heath/dwarf herb** | | Yellow ochre |
| 5 **Dry heath/acid grassland mosaic** | | Orange over yellow ochre |
| 6 **Wet heath/acid grassland mosaic** | | Purple and orange over yellow ochre |
| **E** Mire | | |
| 1 **Bog** | | |
|   *6 **Sphagnum bog** | | |
|     *1 Blanket bog | | Purple |
|     *2 Raised bog | | Purple |
|   *7 Wet modified bog | | Purple |
|   *8 Dry modified bog | | Purple |
| 2 **Flush and spring** | | |
|   1 Acid/neutral flush | | Magenta |
|   2 Basic flush | | Magenta |
|   3 Bryophyte-dominated spring | | Target note |
| *3 **Fen** | | Magenta over purple |
|   Optional codings: | | |
|   Basic | | Magenta over purple |
|   *1 Valley mire | | Magenta over purple |
|   *2 Basin mire | | Magenta over purple |
|   *3 Flood-plain mire | | Magenta over purple |
| *4 **Bare peat** | | Purple |

**F** Swamp, marginal and inundation

1 **Swamp**  Sky blue

2 **Marginal and inundation**

  1 Marginal vegetation  Sky blue + target note

  2 Inundation vegetation  Sky blue

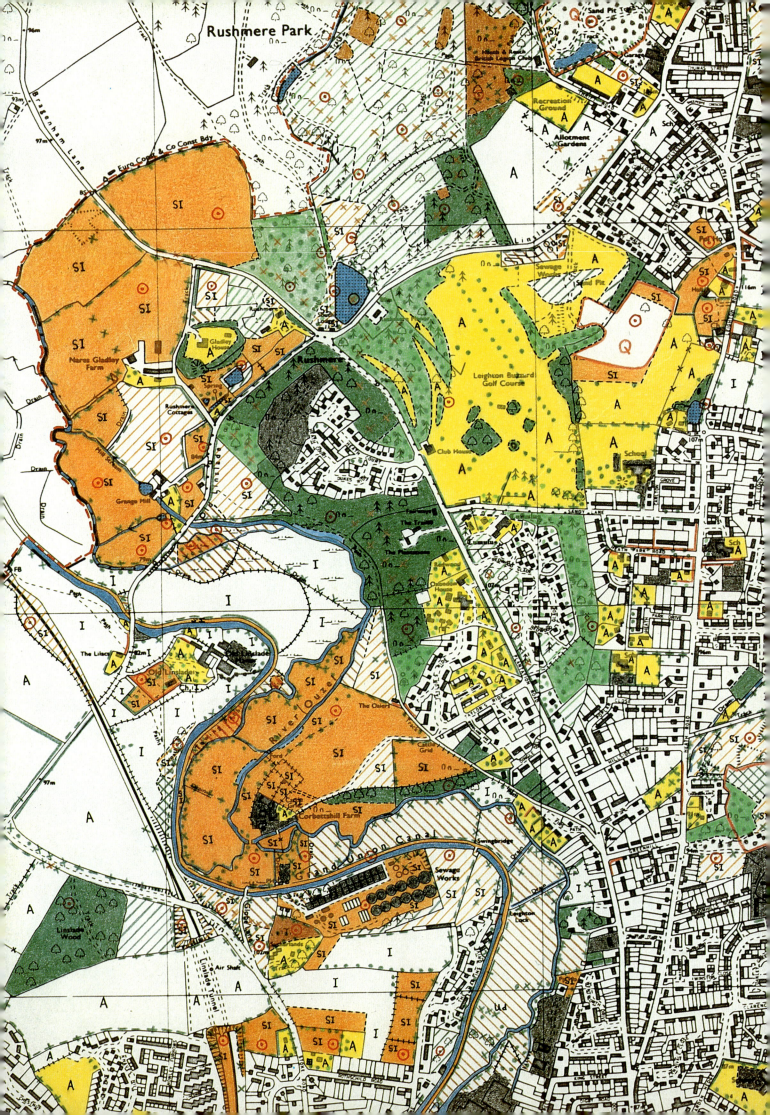

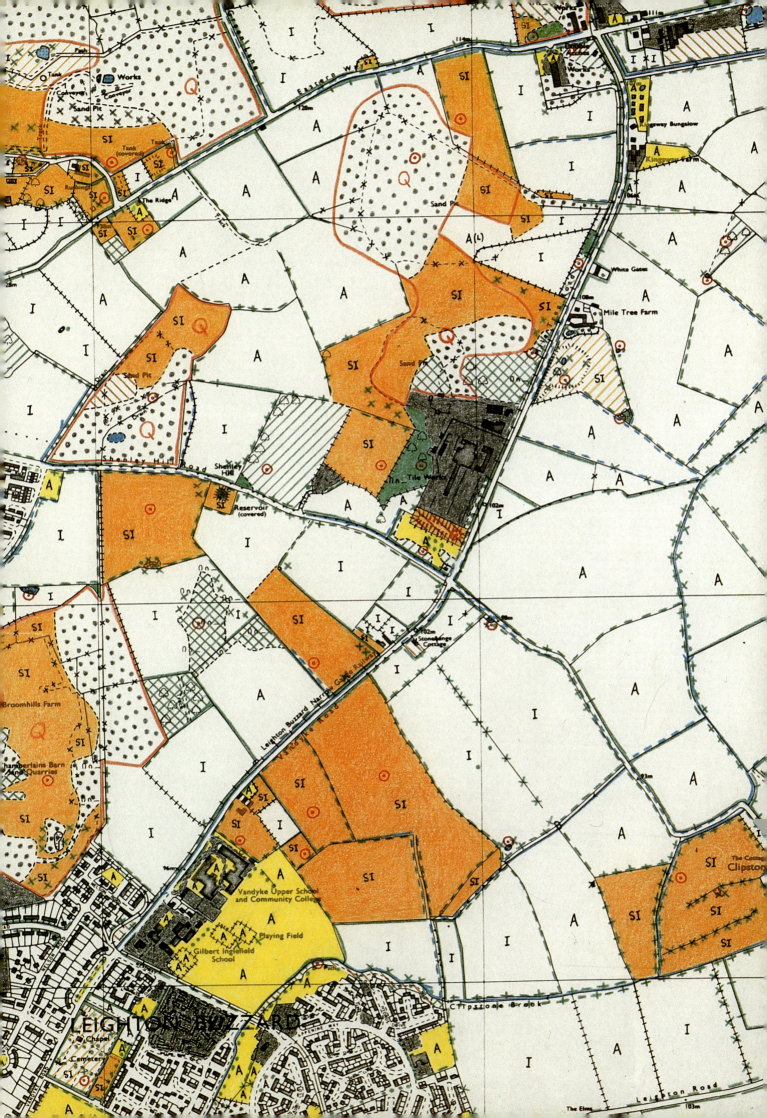

| G | Open water | | |
|---|---|---|---|
| | **1 Standing water** | [blue swatch] | Indigo blue |
| | Optional codings: | | |
| | 1 Eutrophic | E | Indigo blue |
| | 2 Mesotrophic | M | Indigo blue |
| | 3 Oligotrophic | O | Indigo blue |
| | 4 Dystrophic | D | Indigo blue |
| | 5 Marl | C | Indigo blue |
| | 6 Brackish (*includes saline lagoons) | B | Indigo blue |
| | **2 Running water** | [stream symbol] | Indigo blue |
| | Optional codings: | | |
| | 1 Eutrophic | E | |
| | 2 Mesotrophic | M | |
| | 3 Oligotrophic | O | |
| | *4 Dystrophic | D | |
| | *5 Marl/tufa | C | |
| | *6 Brackish | B | |

| H | Coastland | | |
|---|---|---|---|
| | **1 Intertidal** | | |
| | 1 Mud/sand | | Ordnance |
| | 2 Shingle/cobbles | | Survey |
| | 3 Boulders/rocks | | symbols |
| | Codings for intertidal: | | |
| | *1 Zostera beds | Zo | |
| | *2 Green algal beds | Ga | |
| | *3 Brown algal beds | Ba | |
| | **2 Saltmarsh** | | |
| | 3 Saltmarsh/dune interface | [symbol] | Pink + target note |
| | 4 Scattered plants | [symbol] | Pink |
| | *6 Dense continuous | [symbol] | Pink |
| | **3 Shingle above high tide mark** | | Ordnance |
| | **4 Boulders/rocks above high tide mark** | | Survey symbols |
| | **5 Strandline vegetation** | [symbol] | Target note |
| | **6 Sand dune** | | |
| | 4 Dune slack | [swatch] | Indigo blue over flesh |
| | 5 Dune grassland | [swatch] | Orange over flesh |
| | 6 Dune heath | [swatch] | Yellow ochre over flesh |
| | 7 Dune scrub | [swatch] | Green over flesh |
| | *8 Open dune | [swatch] | Flesh |
| | **8 Maritime cliff and slope** | | |
| | 1 Hard cliff | [symbol] | Scarlet red |
| | 2 Soft cliff | [symbol] | Scarlet red |
| | *3 Crevice/ledge vegetation | [symbol] | Target note |
| | *4 Coastal grassland | C | Orange |
| | *5 Coastal heathland | C | Yellow ochre |

| | | | |
|---|---|---|---|
| **I** | **Rock exposure and waste** | | |
| | **1 Natural** | | |
| | 1 Inland cliff | | |
| |    1 Acid/neutral |  | Scarlet red |
| |    2 Basic |  | Scarlet red |
| | 2 Scree | | |
| |    1 Acid/neutral |  | Scarlet red |
| |    2 Basic |  | Scarlet red |
| | 3 Limestone pavement |  | Scarlet red |
| | 4 Other exposure | | |
| |    1 Acid/neutral |  | Scarlet red |
| |    2 Basic |  | Scarlet red |
| | 5 Cave |  | Scarlet red |
| | **2 Artificial** | | |
| | 1 Quarry |  | Scarlet red |
| | 2 Spoil | | Scarlet red |
| | 3 Mine | | Scarlet red |
| | *4 Refuse-tip |  | Scarlet red |

| | | | |
|---|---|---|---|
| **J** | **Miscellaneous** | | |
| | **1 Cultivated/disturbed land** | | |
| | *1 Arable |  | No colour |
| | *2 Amenity grassland |  | Canary yellow |
| | *3 Ephemeral/short perennial |  | Black |
| | *4 Introduced shrub |  | Terra cotta |
| | **2 Boundaries** (mapping optional) | | |
| | 1 Intact hedge | | |
| |    *1 Native species-rich | | Green |
| |    *2 Species-poor | | Green |
| | 2 Defunct hedge | | |
| |    *1 Native species-rich | | Green |
| |    *2 Species-poor | | Green |
| | 3 Hedge and trees | | |
| |    *1 Native species-rich | | Green |
| |    *2 Species-poor | | Green |
| | 4 Fence | | Black |
| | 5 Wall |  | Scarlet red |
| | 6 Dry ditch | | Indigo blue |
| | *7 Boundary removed | | Black |
| | *8 Earth bank | | Black |
| | **3 Built-up areas** | | |
| | 4 Caravan site |  | Black |
| | *5 Sea wall (artificial material) |  | Black |
| | *6 Buildings |  | Black |
| | **4 Bare ground** |  | Black |
| | **5 Other habitat** |  | Black + target note |

## Other mapping aids

| | | |
|---|---|---|
| Target note | ⊙ | Red 0.35 mm Rotring pen |
| Dividing line between habitats where no boundary is marked on the map | --- | Black 0.35 mm Rotring pen |
| Phase 1 survey boundary (delimits area of current field survey) | --- | Red 0.5 mm Rotring pen |
| Habitat information not obtainable because of restricted access | NA | |

## Notes

1  Use only the standard colours in the Berol Verithin series, obtainable from stationers or from Berol Ltd., Oldmeadow Road, King's Lynn, Norfolk, PE30 4JR.

| | | | |
|---|---|---|---|
| VT 01 | Black | VT 46 | Orange |
| VT 05 | Indigo blue | VT 49 | Pink |
| VT 08 | Sky blue | VT 51 | Purple |
| VT 25 | Flesh | VT 55 | Scarlet red |
| VT 31 | Green | VT 66 | Terra cotta |
| VT 32 | True green | VT 89 | Yellow ochre |
| VT 45 | Magenta | VT 80 | Canary yellow |

Shading should be even and fairly light so as not to obscure underlying detail on the printed map, but not so light as to cause difficulty in distinguishing or reproducing the colours. Hatching should be evenly spaced and consistent in direction.

2  Code the dominant species wherever possible, using codes in Appendix 3.

3  *indicates where Phase 1 alphanumeric reference codes differ from those used in either the 1984 NCC/RSNC classification or the 1982 SSSI mapping system (Appendix 7).

4  See Appendix 2 for a comparison of alphanumeric and mnemonic lettered habitat codes.

# Appendix 2

## Habitat codes for use on monochrome field maps and fair maps

|   |   |   |   |   |   | Alphanumeric code | Lettered code |
|---|---|---|---|---|---|---|---|
| A | Woodland and scrub | | | | | | |
| | 1 | Woodland | | | | | |
| | | | Broadleaved | - | semi-natural | A1.1.1 | BW |
| | | | | - | plantation | A1.1.2 | PBW |
| | | | Coniferous | - | semi-natural | A1.2.1 | CW |
| | | | | - | plantation | A1.2.2 | PCW |
| | | | Mixed | - | semi-natural | A1.3.1 | MW |
| | | | | - | plantation | A1.3.2 | PMW |
| | 2 | Scrub | | - | dense/continuous | A2.1 | DS |
| | | | | - | scattered | A2.2 | SS |
| | 3 | Parkland/ scattered trees | | - | broad-leaved | A3.1 | SBW |
| | | | | - | coniferous | A3.2 | SCW |
| | | | | - | mixed | A3.3 | SMW |
| | 4 | Recently-felled woodland | | - | broad-leaved | A4.1 | FB |
| | | | | - | coniferous | A4.2 | FC |
| | | | | - | mixed | A4.3 | FM |
| B | Grassland and marsh | | | | | | |
| | 1 | Acid grassland | | - | unimproved | B1.1 | AG |
| | | | | - | semi-improved | B1.2 | SAG |
| | 2 | Neutral grassland | | - | unimproved | B2.1 | NG |
| | | | | - | semi-improved | B2.2 | SNG |
| | 3 | Calcareous grassland | | - | unimproved | B3.1 | CG |
| | | | | - | semi-improved | B3.2 | SCG |
| | 4 | Improved grassland | | | | B4 | I |
| | 5 | Marsh/marshy grassland | | | | B5 | MG |
| | 6 | Poor semi-improved | | | | B6 | SI |
| C | Tall herb and fern | | | | | | |
| | 1 | Bracken | | - | continuous | C1.1 | CB |
| | | | | - | scattered | C1.2 | SB |
| | 2 | Upland species-rich ledges | | | | C2 | Target note |
| | 3 | Other | | - | tall ruderal | C3.1 | TR |
| | | | | - | non-ruderal | C3.2 | NR |
| D | Heathland | | | | | | |
| | 1 | Dry dwarf shrub heath | | - | acid | D1.1 | ADH |
| | | | | - | basic | D1.2 | BDH |
| | 2 | Wet dwarf shrub heath | | | | D2 | WH |
| | 3 | Lichen/bryophyte heath | | | | D3 | LH |
| | 4 | Montane heath/dwarf herb | | | | D4 | MH |
| | 5 | Dry heath/acid grassland mosaic | | | | D5 | DGM |
| | 6 | Wet heath/acid grassland mosaic | | | | D6 | WGM |

| | | | | | |
|---|---|---|---|---|---|
| E | **Mire** | | | | |
| | 1 Bog | - blanket bog | | E1.6.1 | BB |
| | | - raised bog | | E1.6.2 | RB |
| | | - wet modified | | E1.7 | WB |
| | | - dry modified | | E1.8 | DB |
| | 2 Flush/Spring | - acid/neutral | | E2.1 | AF |
| | | - basic | | E2.2 | BF |
| | | - bryophyte dom. | | E2.3 | Target note |
| | 3 Fen | - valley mire | | E3.1 | VM ) |
| | | - basin mire | | E3.2 | BM ) B where basic |
| | | - flood-plain | | E3.3 | FPM) |
| | 4 Bare peat | | | E4 | P |
| F | **Swamp, marginal and inundation** | | | | |
| | 1 Swamp | | | F1 | SP |
| | 2 Marginal/ inundation | - marginal | | F2.1 | MV |
| | | - inundation | | F2.2 | IV |
| G | **Open water** | | | | |
| | 1 Standing water | - eutrophic | | G1.1 | SWE |
| | | - mesotrophic | | G1.2 | SWM |
| | | - oligotrophic | | G1.3 | SWO |
| | | - dystrophic | | G1.4 | SWD |
| | | - marl | | G1.5 | SWC |
| | | - brackish | | G1.6 | SWB |
| | 2 Running water | - eutrophic | | G2.1 | RWE |
| | | - mesotrophic | | G2.2 | RWM |
| | | - oligotrophic | | G2.3 | RWO |
| | | - dystrophic | | G2.4 | RWD |
| | | - marl | | G2.5 | RWC |
| | | - brackish | | G2.6 | RWB |
| H | **Coastland** | | | | |
| | 1 Intertidal | - mud/sand | | H1.1 | O.S. symbol |
| | | - shingle/cobbles | | H1.2 | O.S. symbol |
| | | - boulders/rocks | | H1.3 | O.S. symbol |
| | | *Zostera* beds | | H1.(1-2).1 | Zo |
| | | green algal beds | | H1.(1-3).2 | Ga |
| | | brown algal beds | | H1.(1-3).3 | Ba |
| | 2 Saltmarsh | - saltmarsh/dune interface | | H2.3 | Target note |
| | | - scattered plants | | H2.4 | SSM |
| | | - dense/continuous | | H2.6 | DSM |
| | 3 Shingle above high tide mark | | | H3 | O.S. symbol |
| | 4 Boulders/rocks above high tide mark | | | H4 | O.S. symbol |
| | 5 Strandline vegetation | | | H5 | Target note |
| | 6 Sand-dune | - dune slack | | H6.4 | DW |
| | | - dune grassland | | H6.5 | DG |
| | | - dune heath | | H6.6 | DH |
| | | - dune scrub | | H6.7 | DX |
| | | - open dune | | H6.8 | OD |
| | 8 Maritime cliff and slope | - hard cliff | | H8.1 | HC |
| | | - soft cliff | | H8.2 | SC |
| | | - crevice/ledge vegetation | | H8.3 | Target note |
| | | - coastal grassland | | H8.4 | SG+target note |
| | | - coastal heathland | | H8.5 | SH+target note |

## I  Rock exposure and waste

### 1  Natural

| | | | |
|---|---|---|---|
| Inland cliff | - acid/neutral | I1.1.1 | AC |
| | - basic | I1.1.2 | BC |
| Scree | - acid/neutral | I1.2.1 | AS |
| | - basic | I1.2.2 | BS |
| Limestone pavement | | I1.3 | LP |
| Other exposure | - acid/neutral | I1.4.1 | AR |
| | - basic | I1.4.2 | BR |
| Cave | | I1.5 | CA |

### 2  Artificial

| | | |
|---|---|---|
| - quarry | I2.1 | Q |
| - spoil | I2.2 | S |
| - mine | I2.3 | MI |
| - refuse-tip | I2.4 | R |

## J  Miscellaneous

### 1  Cultivated/disturbed land

| | | |
|---|---|---|
| - arable | J1.1 | A |
| - amenity grassland | J1.2 | AM |
| - ephemeral/short perennial | J1.3 | ESP |
| - introduced shrub | J1.4 | IS |

### 2  Boundaries

| | | | |
|---|---|---|---|
| Hedges - intact | - species-rich | J2.1.1 | RH |
| | - species-poor | J2.1.2 | PH |
| - defunct | - species-rich | J2.2.1 | RH- |
| | - species-poor | J2.2.2 | PH- |
| - with trees | - species-rich | J2.3.1 | RHT |
| | - species-poor | J2.3.2 | PHT |
| Fence | | J2.4 | F |
| Wall | | J2.5 | W |
| Dry ditch | | J2.6 | DD |
| Boundary removed | | J2.7 | X |
| Earth bank | | J2.8 | EB |

### 3  Built-up areas

| | | |
|---|---|---|
| - caravan site | J3.4 | CS |
| - sea wall | J3.5 | SWALL |
| - buildings | J3.6 | Shade black |

### 4  Bare ground — J4 — BG

### 5  Other habitat — J5 — Target note

## Note

The lettered habitat codes listed in this appendix differ in some respects from the letters overlaid on the colour mapping codes (see Appendix 1).

# Appendix 3
## Dominant species codes

|  |  |
|---|---|
| Ac | *Acer campestre* |
| Ap | *Acer pseudoplatanus* |
| Ah | *Aesculus hippocastanum* |
| Aeu | *Agrimonia eupatoria* |
| At | *Agrostis capillaris (A.tenuis)* |
| Agc | *Agrostis curtisii (A.setacea)* |
| Agt | *Agrostis stolonifera* |
| Aip | *Aira praecox* |
| Ajr | *Ajuga reptans* |
| Aa | *Alchemilla alpina* |
| Alu | *Allium ursinum* |
| Ag | *Alnus glutinosa* |
| Alg | *Alopecurus geniculatus* |
| Ama | *Ammophila arenaria* |
| An | *Anemone nemorosa* |
| As | *Angelica sylvestris* |
| Ao | *Anthoxanthum odoratum* |
| Asy | *Anthriscus sylvestris* |
| Auu | *Arctostaphylos uva-ursi* |
| Ae | *Arrhenatherum elatius* |
| Av | *Artemisia vulgaris* |
| Ast | *Aster tripolium* |
| Aff | *Athyrium filix-femina* |
| Apr | *Avenula pratensis (Helictotrichon pratense)* |
| Apb | *Avenula pubescens (H.elictotrichon pubescens)* |
| Bet | *Betula sp(p)* |
| Bpe | *Betula pendula* |
| Bpu | *Betula pubescens* |
| Bsp | *Blechnum spicant* |
| Bp | *Brachypodium pinnatum* |
| Bs | *Brachypodium sylvaticum* |
| Bm | *Briza media* |
| Be | *Bromus erectus (Zema erecta)* |
| Bxs | *Buxus sempervirens* |
| Ce | *Calamagrostis epigejos* |
| Cac | *Calamagrostis canescens* |
| Cv | *Calluna vulgaris* |
| Cap | *Caltha palustris* |
| Cx | *Carex sp(p)* |
| Cxaa | *Carex acuta* |
| Cxac | *Carex acutiformis* |
| Cxar | *Carex arenaria* |
| Cxb | *Carex bigelowii* |
| Cxe | *Carex elata* |
| Cxf | *Carex flacca* |
| Cxl | *Carex laevigata* |
| Cxn | *Carex nigra* |
| Cxo | *Carex otrubae* |
| Cxpa | *Carex paniculata* |
| Cxrm | *Carex remota* |
| Cxri | *Carex riparia* |
| Cxro | *Carex rostrata* |
| Cxv | *Carex vesicaria* |
| Cb | *Carpinus betulus* |
| Cs | *Castanea sativa* |
| Cn | *Centaurea nigra* |
| Cha | *Chamerion (Chamaenerion) angustifolium* |
| Cop | *Chrysosplenium oppositifolium* |
| Cl | *Circaea lutetiana* |
| Cirs | *Cirsium sp(p)* |
| Car | *Cirsium arvense* |
| Ch | *Cirsium helenioides (C. heterophyllum)* |
| Cp | *Cirsium palustre* |
| Civ | *Cirsium vulgare* |
| Clm | *Cladium mariscus* |
| Com | *Conium maculatum* |
| Cva | *Clematis vitalba* |
| Cos | *Cornus sanguinea (Thelycrania sanguinea)* |
| Ca | *Corylus avellana* |
| Cot | *Cotoneaster sp(p)* |
| Cm | *Crataegus monogyna* |
| Crc | *Crepis capillaris* |
| Cyc | *Cynosurus cristatus* |
| Cys | *Cytisus scoparius (Sarothamnus scoparius)* |
| Dg | *Dactylis glomerata* |
| Dd | *Danthonia decumbens* |
| Dc | *Deschampsia cespitosa* |
| Df | *Deschampsia flexuosa* |
| Dp | *Digitalis purpurea* |
| Do | *Dryas octopetala* |
| Dr | *Dryopteris sp(p)* |
| Ddl | *Dryopteris dilatata* |
| El | *Elymus sp(p)* |
| Ef | *Elymus farctus (Agropyron junceiforme)* |
| En | *Empetrum nigrum* |
| Ep | *Epilobium sp(p)* |
| Eq | *Equisetum sp(p)* |
| Egf | *Equisetum fluviatile* |
| Eqs | *Equisetum sylvaticum* |
| Ec | *Erica cinerea* |
| Et | *Erica tetralix* |
| Erio | *Eriophorum sp(p)* |
| Era | *Eriophorum angustifolium* |
| Ev | *Eriophorum vaginatum* |
| Ee | *Euonymus europaeus* |
| Fs | *Fagus sylvatica* |
| Fo | *Festuca ovina* |
| Fp | *Festuca pratensis* |
| Fr | *Festuca rubra* |
| Fu | *Filipendula ulmaria* |
| Fv | *Fragaria vesca* |
| Fa | *Frangula alnus* |
| Fe | *Fraxinus excelsior* |
| Glt | *Galeobdolon luteum (Lamiastrum galeobdolon)* |
| Gap | *Galium aparine* |
| Gsx | *Galium saxatile* |
| Gp | *Geranium pratense* |
| Gro | *Geranium robertianum* |
| Gs | *Geranium sylvaticum* |
| Gu | *Geum urbanum* |
| Gh | *Glechoma hederacea* |
| Gf | *Glyceria sp(p) (except maxima)* |
| Gm | *Glyceria maxima* |
| Hp | *Halimione portulacoides* |
| Hh | *Hedera helix* |
| Hc | *Helianthemum chamaecistus (H. nummularium)* |
| Hsp | *Heracleum sphondylium* |
| Hr | *Hippophae rhamnoides* |
| Hx | *Holcus sp(p)* |
| Hl | *Holcus lanatus* |
| Hn | *Hyacinthoides non-scripta (Endymion non-scriptus)* |
| Hyp | *Hypericum perforatum* |
| Ia | *Ilex aquifolium* |
| Ig | *Impatiens glandulifera* |
| Ip | *Iris pseudacorus* |
| Ju | *Juncus sp(p)* |
| Ja | *Juncus acutiflorus* |
| Jar | *Juncus articulatus* |
| Je | *Juncus effusus* |
| Ji | *Juncus inflexus* |
| Jm | *Juncus maritimus* |
| Jsq | *Juncus squarrosus* |
| Js | *Juncus subnodulosus* |
| Jt | *Juncus trifidus* |
| Jc | *Juniperus communis* |
| Lx | *Larix sp(p)* |
| Lxd | *Larix decidua* |
| Le | *Lemna sp(p)* |
| Lv | *Leucanthemum vulgare (Chrysanthemum leucanthemum)* |
| Liv | *Ligustrum vulgare* |
| Lvu | *Limonium vulgare* |

| | | | | |
|---|---|---|---|---|
| Lnv | *Linaria vulgaris* | | Sxa | *Salix alba* |
| Lp | *Lolium perenne* | | Sxar | *Salix arbuscula* |
| Lpc | *Lonicera periclymenum* | | Sxau | *Salix aurita* |
| Lzp | *Luzula pilosa* | | Sxc | *Salix caprea* |
| Ls | *Luzula sylvatica* | | Sxci | *Salix cinerea* |
| Lmm | *Lysimachia nummularia* | | Sxf | *Salix fragilis* |
| Md | *Malus domestica* | | Sxh | *Salix herbacea* |
| Maq | *Mentha aquatica* | | Sxl | *Salix lapponum* |
| Mp | *Mercurialis perennis* | | Sxm | *Salix myrsinites* |
| Mc | *Molinia caerulea* | | Sxp | *Salix pentandra* |
| Mym | *Mycelis muralis* | | Sxpu | *Salix purpurea* |
| Mg | *Myrica gale* | | Sxr | *Salix repens* |
| Ns | *Nardus stricta* | | Sxt | *Salix triandra* |
| Nos | *Narthecium ossifragum* | | Sxv | *Salix viminalis* |
| Noth | *Nothofagus* sp. | | Sn | *Sambucus nigra* |
| NuN | *Nuphar/Nymphaea* sp(p) | | Sang | *Sanguisorba officinalis* |
| Nl | *Nuphar lutea* | | Sne | *Sanicula europaea* |
| Na | *Nymphaea alba* | | Saa | *Saxifraga aizoides* |
| Odv | *Odontites verna* | | Slt | *Schoenoplectus (Scirpus) lacustris* |
| Ol | *Oreopteris limbosperma* | | Sl | ssp *lacustris* |
| Oxa | *Oxalis acetosella* | | St | ssp *tabernaemontani* |
| Pas | *Pastinaca sativa* | | Sc | *Schoenus nigricans* |
| Pet | *Petasites hybridus* | | Sv | *Scilla verna* |
| Pha | *Phalaris arundinacea* | | Sm | *Scirpus maritimus* |
| Phl | *Phleum pratense* agg. | | Sno | *Scrophularia nodosa* |
| Pc | *Phragmites australis (P. communis)* | | Sr | *Sedum rosea* |
| Px | *Picea* sp(p) | | Sj | *Senecio jacobaea* |
| Pia | *Picea abies* | | Sea | *Sesleria albicans (Sesleria caerulea)* |
| Pin | *Pinus* sp(p) | | Sia | *Silene acaulis* |
| Psyl | *Pinus sylvestris* | | Sdi | *Silene dioica* |
| Pl | *Plantago lanceolata* | | Sd | *Solanum dulcamara* |
| Pm | *Plantago major* | | Soa | *Sonchus arvensis* |
| Po | *Poa* sp(p) | | Sa | *Sorbus aria* |
| Pbis | *Polygonum bistorta* | | Sac | *Sorbus aucuparia* |
| Pop | *Populus* sp(p) | | Se | *Sparganium erectum* |
| Pot | *Populus tremula* | | Sp | *Spartina* sp(p) |
| Pom | *Potamogeton* sp(p) | | Sph | *Sphagnum* sp(p) |
| Pans | *Potentilla anserina* | | Sme | *Stellaria media* |
| Ppal | *Potentilla palustris* | | Sf | *Suaeda fruticosa* |
| Psn | *Poterium sanguisorba (Sanguisborba minor)* | | Sup | *Succisa pratensis* |
| Pv | *Prunella vulgaris* | | Tb | *Taxus baccata* |
| Pa | *Prunus avium* | | Tsn | *Teucrium scorodonia* |
| Pap | *Prunus avium/padus* | | Til | *Tilia* sp(p) |
| Pnc | *Prunus cerasus* agg. | | Tic | *Tilia cordata* |
| Pdn | *Prunus domestica* | | Tip | *Tilia platyphyllos* |
| Pp | *Prunus padus* | | Tiv | *Tilia vulgaris (Tilia europaea)* |
| Ps | *Prunus spinosa* | | Tc | *Trichophorum cespitosum (Scirpus cespitosus)* |
| Pgm | *Pseudotsuga menziesii* | | Tr | *Trifolium repens* |
| Pt | *Pteridium aquilinum* | | Tff | *Tussilago farfara* |
| Puc | *Puccinellia* sp(p) | | Ty | *Typha* sp(p) |
| Py | *Pyrus* sp(p) | | Ta | *Typha angustifolia* |
| Qu | *Quercus* sp(p) | | Tl | *Typha latifolia* |
| Qp | *Quercus petraea* | | Ul | *Ulex* sp(p) |
| Qr | *Quercus robur* | | Ue | *Ulex europaeus* |
| Rs | *Ranunculus* sp(p) | | Ug | *Ulex gallii* |
| Rfm | *Ranunculus flammula* | | Umi | *Ulex minor* |
| Rr | *Ranunculus repens* | | Um | *Ulmus* sp(p) |
| Rll | *Reseda luteola* | | Umg | *Ulmus glabra* |
| Rj | *Reynoutria japonica* | | Ump | *Ulmus procera* |
| Rl | *Racomitrium lanuginosum* | | Ud | *Urtica dioica* |
| Rc | *Rhamnus catharticus* | | Vm | *Vaccinium myrtillus* |
| Rhin | *Rhinanthus minor* agg. | | Vv | *Vaccinium vitis-idaea* |
| Rp | *Rhododendron ponticum* | | Vd | *Valeriana dioica* |
| Ros | *Rosa* sp(p) | | Vth | *Verbascum thapsus* |
| Rch | *Rubus chamaemorus* | | Vl | *Viburnum lantana* |
| Rf | *Rubus fruticosus* agg. | | Vop | *Viburnum opulus* |
| Ri | *Rubus idaeus* | | Vh | *Viola hirta* |
| Rx | *Rumex* sp(p) | | Vip | *Viola palustris* |
| Ra | *Rumex acetosella* | | Zo | *Zostera* sp(p) |
| Sal | *Salicornia* sp(p) | | Zoa | *Zostera angustifolia* |
| Sx | *Salix* sp(p) | | Zon | *Zostera noltii* |

Group abbreviations

Ba   -   Brown algae (*Fucus* etc in coastal waters)
Brys -   Bryophytes (other than *Sphagnum*)
Cons -   Conifers
Exos -   Exotic shrubs
Ga   -   Green algae (including *Ulva*, *Enteromorpha* and filamentous algae, in saline and fresh waters)
Licn -   Lichens

Notes

1   These codes should be used for mapping dominant species, by superimposing the species code on the appropriate colour code for the habitat (see Appendix 1), where there is sufficient room on the map. The occurrence of dominant species on small areas and non-dominant species of interest should be recorded in target notes.

2   New codes may be devised for any species not given on this list, as long as care is taken to ensure that they do not duplicate existing symbols and the NCC is consulted. New codes should be sent to the England Headquarters, Nature Conservancy Council, Northminster House, Peterborough, PE1 1UA, so that they can be incorporated into the centrally-held master list.

# Appendix 4

## Key words and status categories for target notes

### Key words

| | | | |
|---|---|---|---|
| General | confidential | Damage | afforestation |
| | further Phase 1 survey required | (general) | bracken invasion |
| | Phase 2 survey required | | construction |
| | photograph taken | | deer/rabbit |
| | wildlife corridor | |  damage |
| | | | destruction |
| | | | disturbance |
| Geology/ | acid geology | | drainage |
| topography | chalk | | dumping |
| | clay | | erosion |
| | eroded | | extraction |
| | gravel | | fertiliser |
| | landslide | | fire |
| | limestone | | flood |
| | sand | | overgrazing |
| | sandstone | | herbicide |
| | silt | | liming |
| | steep slope | | peat cutting |
| | soil | | pesticide (other than herbicide) |
| | stability | | pollution |
| | subsidence | | scrub invasion |
| | substratum | | sewage |
| | water table | | silage leachate |
| | | | slurry |
| | | | tree invasion |
| Management | active | | undergrazing |
| (general) | cultivated | | |
| | burnt | | |
| | cut | Flora/ | algae |
| | derelict | fauna | amphibia |
| | disused | | bat |
| | drained | | bird |
| | fenced | | bryophyte |
| | flailed | | butterfly |
| | flooded | | dragonfly |
| | enclosed | | fern |
| | game magement | | fish |
| | stock grazed | | fragmentary vegetation |
| | irrigated | | fungus |
| | mown | | insect |
| | neglected | | introduced species |
| | pest control | | invasive species |
| | restoration | | invertebrate |
| | scrub control | | lichen |
| | tree felling | | mammal |
| | unenclosed | | NVC community |
| | | | orchid |
| Recreation | boating | | reptile |
| | caravans | | seabird |
| | climbing | | species-poor |
| | fishing | | species-rich |
| | footpath | | succession |
| | horse riding | | wader |
| | hunting | | wildfowl |
| | off-road vehicles | | |
| | public pressure | | |
| | shooting | | |
| | skiing | | |
| | walking | | |
| | watersports | | |

## A Woodland and Scrub

- ancient
- boundary bank
- canopy
- carr
- clearing
- coppice
- dead wood
- even age
- fallen trees
- firebreak
- forestry
- ground flora
- high forest
- mixed age
- no regeneration
- orchard
- planted
- pollard
- recent
- regeneration
- rides
- scrubby
- shrub layer
- standard
- underplanted

## B Grassland and Marsh

- alluvial
- ant hills
- hay meadow
- ley
- litter layer
- mole hills
- permanent
- rabbit grazed
- ridge and furrow
- short
- tall
- time of cutting
- water meadow

## C Tall herb and fern

- dry
- mixed
- monospecific
- wet

## D Heathland

- fire break
- grouse moor
- rabbit grazed
- snow bed

## E Mire

- drying
- hagg
- hollow
- hummock
- lagg
- patterned
- pool

## F Swamp, marginal and inundation

- drying
- fluctuating water level
- bare mud
- seasonal
- watertable

## G Open Water

- abstraction
- artificial bank
- canal
- canalised
- dam
- deep
- ditch
- drawdown
- dredged
- fast flow
- fish farming
- fishery
- floating vegetation
- gravel pit
- hydrosere
- island
- lake/loch
- marina
- natural bank
- ornamental
- phytoplanckton bloom
- pond
- reservoir
- riffle
- rocky
- shallow
- slow flow
- submerged vegetation
- tarn
- turbid
- waterfall
- weed cutting

## H Coastland

- accreting
- bait-digging
- coastal defence
- eroding
- machair
- reclamation
- rock pool
- sea wall
- seepage
- spray zone
- stable

## I Rock exposure and waste

- bare (of vegetation)
- coal
- fossil
- gully
- geological interest
- hard
- mineral
- ore
- removal
- soft
- vegetated ledge

## J Miscellaneous

- boundary removed
- cemetery
- churchyard
- construction
- dry ditch
- earth bank
- fallow
- field margin
- garden
- hedge
- industry
- ley
- pipeline
- reseeded
- tunnel
- verge
- wall

## Status categories

### Sites

Ancient monument
AONB (AGLV in Scotland)
Bird sanctuary
Commonland
Country Park
County Trust reserve (including RSNC holdings)
Crown Estate
Forest Nature Reserve
GCR (Geological Conservation Review) site
Heritage Coast
ISR (Invertebrate Site Register) site
LNR (Local Nature Reserve)
MNR (Marine Nature Reserve)
Ministry of Defence
National Scenic Area (Scotland)
National Park
National Trust
NCR (Nature Conservation Review) site
NNR (National Nature Reserve)
Private nature reserve
Public Open Space
Ramsar site
RSPB reserve
SPA (EC Special Protection Area)
SSSI
Wildfowl refuge
Wildlife Scheme
Woodland Trust reserve

### Species

alien
breeding
characteristic
endemic
indicator
rarity – county
 – international
 – local
 – national (Red Data Book)
 – nationally scarce
 – notable
 – regional
 – WCA (Wildlife & Countryside Act Schedules 1, 5 or 8)

# Appendix 5

## Hypothetical examples of target notes

OS Sheet: SK 52 SW

1x1 km grid square: 5122

| | | | |
|---|---|---|---|
| 1 | 510227 | 15.6.83<br>JF, RT | Neutral grassland; unimproved; mown.<br>*Alopecurus pratensis* dominant. Frequent *Orchis morio* and *Primula veris*. Small wet areas with *Caltha palustris*.<br>Owner at adjacent farmhouse. |
| | | 7.80 | Hay meadow card in Scientific File SK52. |
| 2 | 513224 | 13.5.83<br>JF, PK | Scroggs Wood. Broad-leaved, semi-natural wood, coppiced; probably ancient.<br>Dominated by *Quercus robur*. Shrub layer poor: *Corylus*, *Sorbus aucuparia*.<br>Ground flora poor: *Holcus lanatus* and *Deschampsia cespitosa* dominant. *Dryopteris dilatata* and *Trientalis europaea* frequent.<br>Apparently neglected for about 40 years; unenclosed; stock grazed; no regeneration. |
| 3 | 513227 | 18.5.83<br>LW, RT | Blue Tarn. Shallow, oligotrophic standing water with valley mire adjacent.<br>Emergent vegetation dominated by *Juncus* spp and *Menyanthes trifoliata*.<br>Grades into *Sphagnum* + *Eriophorum* bog in the south, and into *Salix* carr in the north.<br>Good for dragonflies, including *Anax imperator* and *Erythromma najas*.<br>Phase 2 survey required; site may warrant special protection. |
| 4 | 515229 | 20.7.83<br>LW, RT | Fragmentary marginal vegetation, occurring along 100 m of the north bank of the river Ugie.<br>Dominant species: *Glyceria plicata* and *Juncus effusus*.<br>Breeding mallard, moorhen and reed bunting. |
| 5 | 517220 | 8.82 | Home Farm pond.<br>Great crested newt - County Wildlife Trust survey, 1982. |

# Appendix 6
## Standard recording forms

### Map sheet record

| Survey title | | | |
|---|---|---|---|
| Map sheet no.* | 10 km sq | Orig. ref. no. | |
| Surveyor(s) | Survey date(s) | | |
| County (counties) | | | |
| L.A. district(s) | | | |
| Area (ha) surveyed | | | |
| Total area (ha) surveyed | Location of records | | |

Notes (include e.g. use of aerial photos, supplementary sources of information, level of detail, habitats and areas omitted)

**Habitat measurements**

| Habitat name | or Standard Phase 1 alphanumeric code | Area (ha) | Length (m) |
|---|---|---|---|
| | | | |

*1:10,000 or 1:25,000 sheet no. or, where measurements are on a 1 km square basis, substitute grid ref.

continued over

| Habitat name | or Standard Phase 1 alphanumeric code | Area (ha) | Length (m) |
|---|---|---|---|
| | | | |

## Target note record

| Survey title | | | Site name | |
|---|---|---|---|---|
| Grid ref. | | 10 km sq | Orig. ref. no. | |
| Surveyor(s) | | | Survey date | |
| Conservation status (if any) | | | SSSI code | |
| County | | L.A. district | | Vice county no. |

| Habitat(s) included | Name | or alphanumeric code |
|---|---|---|
| dominant | | |
| other | | |

Target note (mention supplementary source(s) of information, if used)

Key words by habitat (include management, damage, etc.)

| A Woodland | B Grassland | C Tall herb/fern | D Heathland | E Mire |
|---|---|---|---|---|
| | | | | |

| F Swamp etc. | G Open water | H Coastland | I Rock etc. | J Miscellaneous |
|---|---|---|---|---|
| | | | | |

continued over

| Species recorded

Species name (preferably Latin) | Standard species code | Notes (include habitat code, species status, abundance*) |
|---|---|---|
| Dominant plant species | | |
| Other species of interest (nationally scarce, notable, indicator, etc.) | | |

*Express plant abundance (where not dominant) as abundant/frequent/occasional/rare

# Appendix 7

## The NCC/RSNC habitat classification (revised 1984)

| | First level hierarchy | | Second level hierarchy | | Third level hierarchy | | Fourth level hierarchy |
|---|---|---|---|---|---|---|---|
| A | Woodland and scrub | 1 | Woodland | 1<br>2<br>3 | Broadleaved<br>Coniferous<br>Mixed | 1<br>2 | Semi-natural<br>Plantation |
| | | 2 | Scrub | 1<br>2 | Dense/continuous<br>Scattered | [1<br>[2<br>[3 | Acidic]<br>Neutral]<br>Basic] |
| | | 3 | Parkland and scattered trees | | | | |
| | | 4 | Recently felled woodland | | | | |
| B | Grassland | 1<br>2<br>3 | Acidic<br>Neutral<br>Basic/calcareous | 1<br>2 | Unimproved<br>Semi-improved | 1<br>2 | Upland<br>Lowland |
| | | 4<br>5 | Improved/reseeded<br>Marshy grassland | 1<br>2 | Upland<br>Lowland | | |
| C | Tall herb and fern | 1 | Bracken | 1<br>2 | Continuous<br>Scattered | | |
| | | 2 | Upland spp. - rich vegetation | | | | |
| | | 3 | Other tall herb or fern | 1<br>2 | Ruderal/ephemeral<br>Other | | |
| D | Heathland | 1 | Dry dwarf shrub heath | 1<br>2 | Acidic<br>Basic | 1<br>2 | Upland<br>Lowland |
| | | 2 | Wet dwarf shrub heath | 1<br>2 | Upland<br>Lowland | | |
| | | 3 | Lichen/bryophyte heath | | | | |
| | | 4 | Montane heath/dwarf herb | | | | |
| | | 5 | Dry heath/acidic grass mosaic | | | | |
| | | 6 | Wet heath/acidic grass mosaic | | | | |
| E | Bog and flush | 1 | Bog | 1<br>2<br>3<br>4<br>5 | Blanket bog<br>Upland raised bog<br>Lowland raised bog<br>Valley bog<br>Basin mire | 1<br>2<br>3<br>4<br>5<br>6<br>7<br>8<br>9 | Open *Sphagnum* carpets<br>*Eriophorum vag.* and other bog veg. over *Sphagnum*<br>Mosaic of 1 and 2<br>Bog veg. over *Sphagnum* (no *Eriophorum vag.*)<br>Mosaic of 1 and 4<br>Wet heath over deep peat (no *Sphagnum*)<br>Dry heath over deep peat (no *Sphagnum*)<br>Bare peat<br>Open bog pools |
| | | 2 | Flush | 1<br>2<br>3 | Acidic flush<br>Basic flush<br>Bryophyte-dominated flush | | |
| F | Swamp and fen/inundation communities | 1 | Swamp and fen | 1<br>2 | Single sp. dominant swamp<br>Tall fen vegetation | | |
| | | 2 | Open marginal/inundation communities | 1<br>2 | Fragmentary marginal vegetation<br>Inundation communities | | |

| G | Open water | 1 | Standing water | 1 | Eutrophic | [1 | Small ponds] |
|---|---|---|---|---|---|---|---|
| | | | | 2 | Mesotrophic | [2 | Ponds, etc <0.5 ha] |
| | | | | 3 | Oligotrophic | [3 | Lakes 0.5 ha] |
| | | | | 4 | Dystrophic | [4 | Large lakes > 5 ha] |
| | | | | 5 | Marl | [5 | Canals and ditches] |
| | | | | 6 | Brackish | [6 | Reservoirs] |
| | | 2 | Running water | 1 | Eutrophic | [1 | Spring and small stream <1 m wide] |
| | | | | 2 | Mesotrophic | [2 | Streams and rivers 1-3 m wide] |
| | | | | 3 | Oligotrophic | [3 | Rivers > 3 m wide] |
| | | | | 4 | Marl (5)* | | |
| | | | | 5 | Brackish (6)* | | |
| H | Coastland | 1 | Intertidal | 1 | Mud/sand | 1 | *Zostera* beds (4)* |
| | | | | 2 | Shingle/cobbles | 2 | Green algal beds (5)* |
| | | | | 3 | Boulders/rocks | 3 | Brown algal beds (6)* |
| | | 2 | Saltmarsh | 1 | *Spartina* | | |
| | | | | 2 | Other sp.(p) | | |
| | | | | 3 | Saltmarsh/dune interface | | |
| | | | | 4 | Scattered plants | | |
| | | | | 5 | Inland saltmarsh | | |
| | | 3 | Shingle | | | | |
| | | 4 | Rock/boulders | | | | |
| | | 5 | Strandline vegetation | | | | |
| | | 6 | Sand dune | 1 | Fore dune | | |
| | | | | 2 | Yellow dune | | |
| | | | | 3 | Grey dune | | |
| | | | | 4 | Dune slack | | |
| | | | | 5 | Dune grassland | | |
| | | | | 6 | Dune heath | | |
| | | | | 7 | Dune scrub | | |
| | | 7 | Lagoon | | | | |
| | | 8 | Maritime cliff | 1 | Hard | 1 | Crevice/ledge vegetation (3)* |
| | | | | 2 | Soft | 2 | Seacliff grassland (4)* |
| | | | | | | 3 | Seacliff heath (5)* |
| | | | | | | 4 | Bird cliff vegetation (6)* |
| I | Rock | 1 | Natural rock exposures and caves | 1 | Inland cliff | 1 | Acidic |
| | | | | 2 | Scree | 2 | Basic |
| | | | | 3 | Limestone pavement | | |
| | | | | 4 | Other | 1 | Acidic |
| | | | | 5 | Cave | 2 | Basic |
| | | | | [6 | Mountain top] | | |
| | | | | [7 | Riverine] | | |
| | | | | [8 | Ravine] | | |
| | | 2 | Artificial rock exposures | 1 | Quarry | | |
| | | | | 2 | Spoil heap | | |
| | | | | 3 | Mine | | |
| J | Other | 1 | Cultivated land | | | | |
| | | 2 | Boundary | 1 | Intact hedge | | |
| | | | | 2 | Defunct hedge | | |
| | | | | 3 | Hedgerow with trees | | |
| | | | | 4 | Fence | | |
| | | | | 5 | Wall | | |
| | | | | 6 | [Dry] Ditch | | |
| | | | | (7)** | | | |
| | | 3 | Building | 1 | Agricultural (incl. forestry) | | |
| | | | | 2 | Industrial | | |
| | | | | 3 | Domestic | | |
| | | | | 4 | Caravans | | |
| | | 4 | Bare ground | | | | |
| | | 5 | Others | | | | |
| K | Marine | | | | | | |

**Note**
This classification is very similar to the 1982 NCC SSSI habitat mapping system, (which follows the 1982 version of the NCC/RSNC classification). The differences are indicated on the table thus:-

[ ] = Not included in the SSSI habitat mapping system.
* = Numbered differently in the SSSI habitat mapping system - the SSSI number codes in parentheses.
J(7)** = Boundary removed - an additional category in the SSSI habitat mapping system.

# Appendix 8

## Relationship between Phase 1 habitat categories and National Vegetation Classification communities

|   |   |   |   | NVC communities associated with (but not necessarily confined to) habitat categories |
|---|---|---|---|---|
| A | **Woodland and scrub** | | | |
| | 1 Woodland | | | |
| | | Broadleaved | - semi-natural | W4-12, 14-17 |
| | | | - plantation | - |
| | | Coniferous | - semi-natural | W13 and 18 |
| | | | - plantation | - |
| | | Mixed | - semi-natural | W1-18 |
| | | | - plantation | - |
| | 2 Scrub | | | W1-3, 19-25 |
| | 3 Parkland/scattered trees | | | Appropriate grassland type with scattered trees |
| | 4 Recently-felled woodland | | | - |
| B | **Grassland and marsh** | | | |
| | 1 Acid grassland | - unimproved | | U1-6 |
| | | - semi-improved | | U1-6 |
| | 2 Neutral grassland | - unimproved | | MG1-5, 8-10 |
| | | - semi-improved | | MG1, 3-6, 11 |
| | 3 Calcareous grassland | - unimproved | | CG1-14 |
| | | - semi-improved | | CG1-13 |
| | 4 Improved grassland | | | MG6 and 7 |
| | 5 Marsh/marshy grassland | | | MG8 and 10, M22-28 |
| | 6 Poor semi-improved grassland | | | MG6 |
| C | **Tall herb and fern** | | | |
| | 1 Bracken | | | U20 |
| | 2 Upland species-rich ledges | | | U17 |
| | 3 Other | - tall ruderal | | Not available |
| | | - non-ruderal | | Various, including U16 and 19 |
| D | **Heathland** | | | |
| | 1 Dry dwarf shrub heath | - acid | | H1-6, 8-10, 12-22 |
| | | - basic | | H7, 8, 10 |
| | 2 Wet dwarf shrub heath | | | M15 and 16 |
| | 3 Lichen/bryophyte heath | | | H1 and 11, U1 and 10, SD13 |
| | 4 Montane heath/dwarf herb | | | U7-10, H13 |
| | 5 Dry heath/acid grassland mosaic | | | Mixtures |
| | 6 Wet heath/acid grassland mosaic | | | Mixtures |

**E  Mire**

    1  Bog    - blanket bog                       M2, 17-20
                  - raised bog                         M17-20
                  - wet modified bog               M20 and 25
                  - dry modified bog               M19 and 20

    2  Flush/  - acid/neutral                    M4-7, 21, 29, ?14
        Spring  - basic                          M10-13, 34-36, ?14
                 - bryophyte-dominated       M32, 37, 38

    3  Fen    - valley mire                      M4, 6, 7, 10-14, 17, 21, 29, 30
                  - basin mire                       S24-28, M4-9
                  - flood-plain mire                S24-28, M4-9

    4  Bare peat                                   -

**F  Swamp, marginal and inundation**

    1  Swamp                                       S1-22, 27, 28

    2  Marginal and inundation    - marginal        S1-28
                                            - inundation       Various, including MG13

**G  Open water**                                       Various mixtures

**H  Coastland**

    1  Intertidal  - mud/sand                   SM1-3
                          - shingle/cobbles          -
                          - boulders/rocks            -

    2  Saltmarsh                                    SM1-22

    3  Shingle above high-tide mark           SD1-5

    4  Rocks/boulders above high-tide mark   MC1-7

    5  Strandline vegetation                    SD1-4

    6  Sand-dune   - dune slack                   SD15 and 16
                          - dune grassland           SD9, 10-12
                          - dune heath                 Various, including
                                                          H10 and 11, M15 and 16
                          - dune scrub                  SD17
                          - open dune                   SD2, 5-14

    8  Maritime cliff   - hard cliff                   -
        and slope        - soft cliff                    -
                              - crevice/ledge vegetation   MC1-4
                              - coastal grassland          MC5-12 and various grassland communities
                              - coastal heathland          Various, especially H7 and 11